ATHEISM AND ALIENATION

ATHEISM
AND
ALIENATION

A Study of the Philosophical Sources
of Contemporary Atheism

PATRICK MASTERSON, Ph.D.

GILL AND MACMILLAN

Published by
GILL AND MACMILLAN LTD
2 Belvedere Place
Dublin 1

and in London through association with
MACMILLAN AND CO LTD

7171 0501 6

Cover design by Cor Klaasen

Printed and bound in the Republic of Ireland by
CAHILL & CO LIMITED DUBLIN 8

To my mother

and the memory of my father

Contents

vii

Preface

THE affirmation of God is undoubtedly one of the most noteworthy of human achievements. In its various historical expressions it speaks profoundly of man's appraisal of his own condition—of his perfection and weakness, of his ideals and failures, of his hopes and fears. It symbolises in a most striking fashion his endeavour to make sense both of his aspirations and of his limitations.

However, scarcely less remarkable an achievement is man's repudiation of this affirmation of God. Atheism in its various forms, no less than theism, is a most significant expression of man's representation of himself to himself. Indeed, inasmuch as it proposes itself as a post-theistic phenomenon, it professes to convey a more reflective and authentic image of man than that portrayed in any version of theism.

This phenomenon of atheism can be considered from a variety of viewpoints, each characterised by its own principles and aims. Thus a theologian, a psychologist, a sociologist and a political economist would each advance different, though not necessarily incompatible, expositions of the significance of atheism. It is not the purpose of this study to present a survey of such particular approaches. It aims rather to provide a more basic account of the general significance of contemporary atheism through an elucidation of its philosophical evolution. In effect, it seeks to trace the philosophical milestones in the development of contemporary atheism from its origins in modern thought to the present day.

The universally acknowledged crucial significance of the Cartesian *cogito* in the formation of modern self-understanding is a guiding motif of the study. It seeks to show how the viewpoint of the *cogito*, reinforced by the impact of modern science, has inspired the philosophical itinerary in the course of which the traditional conviction that the alienated man is the man who does not believe in God has given way to the view that belief in God is a profound source of human alienation. This theme is illustrated in its development in the philosophies of Kant, Hegel, Feuerbach and Marx, and in its contemporary expression in positivistic Naturalism and Existentialism.

What emerges in the course of this study is the elaboration of a humanism of liberty which calls in question the possibility of the coexistence of finite and infinite being—or, more concretely, the coexistence of man and God. How can the ever more impressive claims of human subjectivity to be an irreducible source of a world of meaning and value be rendered compatible with the claims involved in the theistic conception of God as absolute creator of all finite being? The story of the development of contemporary atheism is unfolded as a progressive repudiation not only of a theistic absolute but also of every secular substitute such as the absolute spirit of Hegel, the social absolute of Feuerbach and Marx, or the scientific absolutism of Positivism.

Inevitably a work of this scope must be selective in its treatment of themes and sources. Thus, even within its limited horizon of modern and contemporary European thought, it does not consider explicitly many philosophers who have elaborated important reflections on the problem of God. It seeks simply to mediate insight, through certain key philosophical illustrations, into the basic themes which have animated the development of contemporary atheism.

In portraying this development, it strives for simplicity of expression without lapsing into superficiality of presentation. Arising out of the account of this development, certain positive suggestions concerning the problem of God today are advanced in the final chapter.

This book originated from a series of lectures to undergraduate students of philosophy. To facilitate such readers' further investigation of the topics discussed, references are, where possible, to standard English language versions of works cited. I would like to thank my colleagues in the Faculty of Philosophy of University College, Dublin, whose ideas and interest have been of value to me in writing this book, especially Professor J. Horgan, Dr D. Connell, Dr S. Samay, Dr P. Pettit and Mr D. Turner. I wish also to acknowledge my debt to the editors of *Philosophical Studies, Atlantis,* and *Studies,* in which some of the material of chapters 3–5 first appeared. Finally, I would like to thank my wife Frances for providing the domestic *ambiance* and practical encouragement which did so much to make the whole enterprise possible.

January, 1971.   PATRICK MASTERSON.

I

Modern Science and the Cartesian Cogito

To a large extent the emphasis of contemporary atheism has shifted from a critique of the proofs for the *existence* of God to a rejection of the *properties* traditionally attributed to Him. More fundamentally it might be said that the atheism of our day, in its reflective philosophical expression, consists chiefly in asserting the impossibility of the coexistence of finite and infinite being. It is maintained that the affirmation of God as infinite being necessarily implies the devaluation of finite being and, in particular, the dehumanisation of man. The merely negative form of atheism has been replaced by a more sophisticated version according to which contemporary man if he is to be truly human must, perhaps reluctantly, dispense with belief in God.

Thus the 'problem of God' is posed today as a feature of a more basic problem of human alienation and authenticity. The debate revolves around the following kind of questions—'Is the presence of God constitutive of man's historical existence or destructive of it? In order that a man may exist, "stand forth" as a man in freedom and in human action, what is required—that he recognise and acknowledge the presence of God, as the Old and New Testaments say, or that he ignore and refuse God's presence, as the Revolution and the Theatre say? In order that the people may exist, organised for action in history as a force to achieve a historical destiny, what is required—that they disown

God or own themselves to be his people? What is it that alienates man from himself—the confession of God's presence in history and in man's consciousness or the suppression of him from history and the repression of him from consciousness?"[1]

This theme of alienation is fundamental to a consideration of the development of contemporary atheism. For today on an ever increasing scale people proclaim themselves to be atheists, not so much because of objections to alleged proofs for the existence of God but rather because they consider that to affirm the existence of God is to set men at odds within themselves and with one another. The widespread currency of this conviction is a revealing illustration of a new 'world-view' which has been articulating itself throughout the past few centuries and which now constitutes an axiomatic framework or cultural atmosphere within which we deploy our quest for meaning, value and authenticity in our experience and our life.

In previous ages prior to the development of positive science, the emergence of modern philosophy, the birth of the revolutionary ideology of democracy and the growth of industrial city life, quite the opposite view prevailed. In a basically agricultural epoch man lived out his life as though in an objectively ordered universe whose meaning and value presented itself as somehow already there before man and independent of him. He lived in a world with its own pre-determined order to which he had to learn to conform or perish. The forces and laws of Nature, more ancient than man himself, assumed a quasi-sacred character and appeared as the model for the organisation of both his individual and his social life. His world was one in which everything had been accomplished from all eternity, a divinely ordered world, fundamentally devoid of novelty. The hierarchical order and constant rhythm of the cosmos, which so intimately determined the agricultural activities of man, appeared as absolutely given rather than humanly constituted, and thereby facilitated the affirmation of a divine source. The world as an immediate epiphany of hierarchically ordered being proclaimed the reality and glory of a comprehensive divine wisdom and power.

In such a cultural context, permeated by a lively sense of the sacred, it was readily accepted that the alienated man, the estranged man, was the man who did not believe in God or who did not live out the consequences of belief in God. Only through lived fidelity to divine providence could man achieve inner harmony, reconciliation, and fulfilment. 'Thou hast made us for thyself O Lord and our hearts are restless until they rest in thee' (St Augustine). The man who denied God was not the mature, sophisticated, well-integrated man. On the contrary he was the irrational, morally disorientated and foolish man. 'The fool says in his heart, "There is no God!"' (*Ps.* 14:1). The unbelievers who explored the beauty and order of the cosmos and, notwithstanding the palpable and overwhelming evidence readily accessible to them, failed to recognise its divine source were fools who 'live in darkness and the shadow of death' (*Luke* 1:79). In their barren and idolatrous speculations about the universe 'they made nonsense out of logic and their empty minds were darkened' (*Rom.* 1:21).

At the level of community no less than at the level of individual existence acknowledgement of God was the basic source of unity, harmony and peace. Just as it was their trust in the faithful presence of Yahweh that welded the Israelite tribes into a unified people, so likewise it was faith in the Christian God which was the touchstone of medieval society. It was the age not simply of Christianity but of Christendom. Its ideology was a theology. A theological synthesis provided the unifying framework for the various spheres of knowledge, culture and the organisation of society.

Undoubtedly many of the medieval theologians and philosophers made important distinctions between reason and faith, grace and nature, the sacred and the secular. Likewise, they developed profound reflections concerning the intrinsic intelligibility and relative autonomy of the created order. But the cultural context within which such reflections were developed was an unquestioned theistic context pre-reflectively animated and pervasively informed by Christian faith. Moreover, their goal was the intellectual integration of all reality into a unified Christian order. As one commentator remarks: 'It is important to grasp that the development of the Christian culture fused the concerns of heaven and earth, of nature and of history, into one dependable order. In spite of the widely recognised diversity in the middle ages, its single thrust was the unity of all things, with everything having its appropriate place. The feudal order, the order of church and empire, the order of the heavens, for all their distinctions, are considered analogous to each other and finally reflect one order, the kingdom itself.'[2]

Speaking very generally, one might say that until a new conception of man and of nature began to develop in the sixteenth and seventeenth centuries, a conception still in the making today, man found his identity, meaning and purpose, both as an individual and as a member of society, in terms of a sacred world-view. It was a world-view which located the place and the purpose of man within a comprehensive divine plan. At all events, any suggestion that belief in God disorientated man within himself and *vis-à-vis* his fellow-men would have appeared exceedingly paradoxical within this world-view.

The emergence of the attitude which correlates belief in God with the theme of human alienation was inaugurated in large measure by the development of positive science. The growth of positive science under the inspiration of men of genius such as Copernicus (1473–1543), Galileo (1564–1642), and especially Newton (1642–1727), disclosed a radically new way of considering and understanding the physical universe. It displaced the traditional well-defined notion of a hierarchical finite cosmos fostered such ready acceptance of supraterrestrial, and divine realities. It proposed in its place an infinite, uniform, mechanical universe rry heavens above were no more intrinsically mysterious or sublime than the sands of the shore underfoot. Thus the historian Butterfield observes: 'A universe constructed on the mechanics of Aristotle had the door half-way open for spirits already; it was a universe in which unseen hands had to be in constant operation, and sublime Intelligences had to roll the planetary spheres around. Alternatively, bodies had to be endowed with souls and aspirations, with a "disposition" to certain kinds of motion, so that matter itself seemed to possess mystical qualities. The modern law of inertia, the modern theory of motion, is the great factor which in the seventeenth century helped to drive the spirits out of the world and opened the way to a universe that ran like a piece of clockwork.'[3]

With the advent of modern science, mathematics, not metaphysics, imposed itself as the appropriate language in which to formulate a scientific and experimental understanding of the world. The new science, in its mature development, did not derive its laws from metaphysical considerations or present itself as essentially subordinate to and requiring integration and completion within a system of metaphysics and natural theology. In its inner logic it aspired to the status of an autonomous discipline erected independently upon its own distinctive fundamental axioms. It encouraged the ideal of understanding the universe simply from within itself rather than in terms of some external spiritual or divine principle. It aimed specifically at achieving a scientific understanding of the world precisely from within the world. Any reference to God or to angels as the cause of what goes on in the world was beyond the proper frame of reference of the new scientific viewpoint. Any such reference would involve a misconception of the level of intelligibility which it sought and the methods whereby it hoped to attain this intelligibility—even though admittedly it was some time before this fact was duly appreciated even by scientists themselves. The only kind of hypothesis appropriate to the new scientific attitude was one which could

B

in principle be verified or discredited by empirical observation or experiment. Quite clearly an appeal to God whom 'no man hath seen at any time' would be the paradigm of what could not feature as a genuine hypothesis in this context.

The understandable historical tension between the traditional and the new scientific conceptions of the world contained the seeds of bitter theological and philosophical controversy which, as we shall see presently, blossomed into various forms of philosophical positivism according to which the affirmation of God is incompatible with an integral scientific outlook. The stage was set for the view that the affirmation of God constituted an estrangement and alienation from the inner dynamism of man's most decisive achievement, namely, a truly scientific mentality.

It should of course be borne in mind that the explicit assertion of this view was achieved only gradually. Indeed, in general, the outstanding pioneers of modern science, men such as Boyle and Newton, were convinced that their speculations confirmed beyond doubt the existence of God. They believed that the existence of a provident God was absolutely required in order to ensure that the great cosmic clock was properly set and kept in good working order. It was some time before the intrinsically *a*-theistic character of the new conception of the world and of the scientific method which sustained it became apparent. But gradually any reference to God became increasingly remote and incidental in the scientific explanation of the world. Eventually He became irrelevant even to an account of the origin and maintenance of the solar system and was lost in vague hypothetical speculations about the source of a pre-solar nebula. The dominant focus of interest became the exclusively natural explanation of all physical phenomena. As one writer describes the development: 'the mighty, energetic God of Newton who actually "ran" the universe according to His free will and decision, became in quick succession, a conservative power, an *intelligentia supra-*

mundana, a "Dieu fainéant". Laplace who, a hundred years after Newton, brought the New Cosmology to its final perfection, told Napoleon, who asked him about the role of God in his *System of the World:* "Sire, je n'ai pas eu besoin de cette hypothèse." But it was not Laplace's *System,* it was the world described in it that no longer needed the hypothesis God.'[4]

People affected by the cultural resonance of the new scientific world-view would no longer accept the existence of God as a matter of course. Others would dismiss belief in His existence as a form of pre-scientific superstition. Admittedly, on careful consideration, none of the great bulwarks of the new conception of the universe such as the heliocentric theory, the law of inertia, or the law of gravitation, can be shown to be in principle incompatible with the affirmation of God. But the views which they replaced were so inextricably bound up with the affirmation of God and a variety of theological themes that for many people their downfall tended to undermine the affirmation of God rather than facilitate a more authentic and purified understanding of His nature. Likewise, strictly speaking the methodological *a*-theism of the modern scientific viewpoint simply put the question of God's existence out of play. However, it also generated a frame of mind which tended to generalise its methodological indifference to the divine into an absolute scientific humanism.

Thus the development of positive science, which so dramatically transformed our cognitional horizon, must be counted as a factor of central significance in the formation of contemporary atheism. It paved the way for persistent currents of philosophical empiricism, materialism, and positivism. Moreover, it presented such a new diagram of the physical universe that in seeking his bearings man could raise in concrete terms the possibility that in the theocentric world, which he previously inhabited as though at home, he was in fact lost and alienated from his true foundations.

Concomitant with the growth of positive science, and in part inspired by its disclosure of the creative virtuosity of human enquiry, there developed a new confidence and critical interest in the intrinsic resources and scope of the human mind. The world as portrayed by science, in contrast with the commonplace world of ordinary experience, appeared to derive its intelligible structure from the mathematical ingenuity of man. Hence, attention came to be focused on the question of the contribution of the knowing subject to the object of his knowledge. This development is well illustrated in the thought of Descartes (1596–1650) who is generally hailed as the founder of modern philosophy. In his writings we witness the emergence of a special interest in subjectivity—an interest which has animated the subsequent history of philosophy and which is an essential feature in the story of contemporary atheism. As Professor Fabro in his monumental study of modern atheism observes: 'In antiquity and, indeed, right down to the point at which modern thought emerges, atheism represented a sporadic phenomenon occurring within the confines of a cultural élite, but as soon as the *cogito* comes on the scene atheism assumes an all-embracing structure simultaneously invading public life and individual behaviour.'[5]

At first sight it may strike one as odd to see the thought of Descartes described as a significant source of atheism. For the man himself was a convinced Christian and he considered his whole philosophy to be a most powerful defence of theism. Indeed the idea of God, from which is derived the affirmation of His existence, is an utterly indispensable feature of his philosophical system. Nevertheless, we must distinguish between the intentions and even the explicit assertions of a thinker on the one hand, and the implicit logic of his method and his principles on the other. That the latter in Descartes' case are a fertile source of atheism is amply illustrated by the subsequent course of philosophical reflection which drew inspiration from his genius.

Stated very simply, Descartes' philosophical revolution

consisted in calling in question (albeit only provisionally) the reality of the external world and directing man's quest for a basic framework of meaning, certitude, and value, inwards to the resources of his own subjectivity rather than outwards to a divinely formed external world immediately given in sensible experience. More precisely, Descartes inaugurated the reign of the principle of immanentism which has dominated the evolution of modern philosophy. This principle repudiates the traditional epistemological position according to which being enjoys primacy *vis-à-vis* thought in such a manner that it is the self-revelation or epiphany of being itself which grounds thought as consciousness of being. Instead, in virtue of a programme of radical doubt, the principle of immanentism involutes the direction of consciousness and prescribes that it takes as its only and absolute starting point the luminous presence of the thinking subject to himself—a subject defined as identical with his own thought. Hence the only access which there is to being is through the *cogito*'s excogitation of himself. Thought assumes primacy *vis-à-vis* being which henceforth is grounded in the self-sufficiency and luminous presence of the thinking self to himself. This presence of the thinking self to himself becomes the first principle and ultimate foundation from which all validity, certitude and value must in some way be derived. Whatever being comes to be affirmed is affirmed from within and as a determination of this self-sufficient closed circuit of thought.

The new philosophical perspective inaugurated by Descartes, which aspires to originate all epistemology and ontology from within an intellectual intuition of the self as thought, has in various ways been the central inspiration of subsequent philosophical reflection.[6] What is of particular interest to our discussion is the fact that it also provided a philosophical framework in which the modern problematic of atheism and alienation could be formulated. It suggested a speculative viewpoint in terms of which one could contest the traditional theological assertion that sin and estrangement arise from a deflection of our primary concern and interest from God to self. For henceforth whatsoever might appear to relativise Descartes' new and seemingly exalted conception of man as an autonomous *cogito* could be construed as a source of alienation which must be transcended. It could be seen as tending to understand man in terms of the other than man and forgetting that any affirmation of the other than man is contextually dependent upon and radiates forth from man as an englobing milieu of thought. The affirmation of a transcendent God as a first principle more fundamental than the *cogito* would pose this problem of alienation in a concrete and radical manner. The chief contours of contemporary atheism, understood as a calling in question of the possible coexistence of distinct orders of finite and infinite being, would be prefigured in the tension between the affirmations of the primacy of the *cogito* on the one hand and the primacy of a transcendent God on the other. In Descartes we find not only the first affirmation but also, as we shall now see, the second. Thus, through an inherent ambiguity in his thought, in virtue of which he personally eludes the problem of atheism, he adumbrates the essential elements of this problem for future generations.

We have indicated how Descartes attributed an unprecedented autonomy and primacy to man understood as a *cogito* who triumphs over doubt and illusion and who from within his own resources as a thinking being originates a comprehensive order of solidly established truth. However, this autonomy is at once qualified by Descartes in such a radical manner that the coherence of his system is imperilled. For he proceeds directly to an affirmation of God as the indispensable ground of certain truth. 'I must inquire whether there is a God as soon as the occasion presents itself; and if I find that there is a God, I must also inquire whether He may be a deceiver; for without a knowledge of these two truths I do not see that I can ever be certain of anything.'[7]

From his *idea* of God as infinite, eternal, independent,

omniscient, supremely perfect and omnipotent being, he passes directly to the affirmation of God's existence. With this affirmation a switch of perspective occurs and God becomes the first principle of philosophical thought. The objective idea of God is accorded a positivity and a primacy even *vis-à-vis* the finite *cogito*'s perception of himself. 'Nor should I imagine that I do not perceive the infinite by a true idea, but only by the negation of the finite, just as I perceive repose and darkness by the negation of movement and of light; for, on the contrary, I see that there is manifestly more reality in infinite substance than in finite, and therefore that in some way I have in me the notion of the infinite earlier than the finite—to wit, the notion of God before that of myself.'[8]

It soon transpires that the finite *cogito* is not the absolute or creative source of the truths and values which it affirms. It merely assents to an order of truth and value which it discerns in itself as deriving from a more fundamental principle, namely, the divine Will. The sovereign freedom of man, which from within man's own resources as a thinking being accomplishes the disclosure of an order of truth and value, and which at times Descartes even describes as infinite, is seen in the last analysis to be merely freedom on the one hand to avoid error and deception, i.e. to refuse non-being, and on the other hand to assent to a divinely ordained scheme of things. The dramatic prospect of radical autonomy intimated in Descartes' original swing to subjectivity collapses into utter subjection to the blinding light of an order of truth and value deriving their whole reality from God's creative freedom. 'For as often as I so restrain my will within the limits of my knowledge that it forms no judgement except on matters which are clearly and distinctly represented to it by the understanding, I can never be deceived; for every clear and distinct conception is without doubt something, and hence cannot derive its origin from what is nought, but must of necessity have God as its author.'[9]

In a penetrating evaluation of Cartesian thought the contemporary existentialist philosopher J. P. Sartre argues that Descartes failed to carry through his exploration of human subjectivity when, having realised that truth must be ultimately grounded in absolutely autonomous and creative freedom, he attributed this truth and its productive grounding freedom to God rather than to man.[10] Sartre claims that in so doing Descartes was guilty of sublimation and transposition and perpetrated an obvious alienation of man from himself. The principle which is the essential basis of humanism, namely, that man is the being whose advent makes a world exist, still remained to be definitively worked out. Descartes' revolutionary philosophy opened the way to this new perspective, brought us well along the road, but finally, at the price of considerable ambiguity and even inconsistency, remained faithful to a theocentric viewpoint.

Since Descartes' pioneering efforts, the course of culture and philosophy has witnessed to a progressive triumph of subjectivity which has posed in increasingly acute terms the problem of the relationship between alienation and religious belief. Following Sartre's clue in the course of his reflections on Descartes' philosophy, it may be said that the new world-view which has been spelling itself out steadily over the past few centuries is essentially the emergence of a new humanism of liberty, a new way of understanding the meaning of man, society, and history. In effect, man is becoming progressively more aware of all that his liberty signifies and of his intrinsic power to fashion and control the factors influencing his life. Through the exploration of his subjectivity, through his quest for forms of social life which would respect and foster the aspirations of this subjectivity, and through the empirical witness at the level of scientific and technological achievements to the claims of this subjectivity to shape the course of history, man has worked relentlessly towards a new self-understanding of his condition. As this new self-understanding developed, the affirmation of God was no longer automatically accepted as the unifying and utterly basic principle of man's integrity, meaning and value. Rather, with increasing emphasis, it tended to appear as something alien, threatening and dehumanising.

This new viewpoint, this humanism of liberty, congealed into a coherent pattern in the course of the eighteenth and nineteenth centuries. The traditional theological imagery of revolt entailing alienation and enslavement as depicted, for example, in the revolt of the fallen angels, the revolt of Adam, the tower of Babel, the revolt of Prometheus, the Augustinian city of man, was transformed into an ideology of revolution promising integration and liberation. This new ideology took on flesh and blood at the economic level in the concrete form of the industrial revolution, at the social and political levels in the concrete form of the American, and—even more notably—French, revolutions, at the speculative level in the concrete form of the Copernican revolution of Kant's philosophy. It is to the central theoretical significance of Kant's philosophy in the development of contemporary atheism that we must now turn our attention.

2

Kant and the Finite Absolute

In the thought of Immanuel Kant (1724–1804) one discerns a new stage in man's philosophical account of his own meaning and value, and a new appraisal of the relationship between man and God. He develops Descartes' emphasis on subjectivity towards an unequivocal affirmation of the autonomy of man. Thus, whereas for Descartes man merely discovers truth as something divinely pre-established, according to Kant he *constitutes* it in virtue of his own intrinsic resources.

Kant sought to refute what he considered to be the inadequate views of both post-Cartesian rationalists such as Leibniz and Wolff and post-Cartesian empiricists such as Locke and Hume. To this end he developed in detail an original philosophical defence of truth and value which instead of seeking their foundation in a transcendent God sought it rather within the transcendental dimensions of the human spirit itself. He grounded the universality and necessity of science and the absoluteness of moral values, not in the mind and will of God, but rather in the *a priori* forms of man's own understanding and the autonomy of man's pure practical reason. He developed the ideal of a metaphysics of finitude—an ideal which still inspires the speculation of much of contemporary philosophy.

A basic problem which confronted Kant, and one to which his philosophy is in part a proposed solution, was the problem of vindicating the claims of mathematics and natural science in the face of the radical scepticism of the great empiricist philosopher David Hume (1711–1776). Drawing the principles of empiricism to their ultimate conclusion Hume argued that if all we know directly are discrete sense impressions then it is futile to seek any theoretical justification for a scientific conception of the world. If knowledge is reducible to atomic impressions such as those of colour, sound, texture and shape, no foundation can be adduced for the affirmation of necessary and universal truths about physical objects. More assuredly still, no foundation can be adduced for the affirmations of traditional metaphysics about realities which transcend any possible sensible experience such as the world as a whole, the soul and God.

In view of its disunited and inconclusive condition Kant readily conceded the dubious character of the claims of metaphysics. However, he insisted that in the light of the achievements of modern scientists such as the incomparable Newton, no reasonable person could seriously deny that we do in fact possess scientific knowledge of physical objects. Hence he proposed in his *Critique of Pure Reason* to determine the conditions which must obtain in order to render possible this scientific knowledge which is unquestionably possible.[1] In the light of these considerations he hoped to attain a purified critical understanding of the knowing subject which would enable him to decide whether or not man was capable of any valid metaphysical knowledge of realities such as God.

According to Kant, to ask what are the conditions which make science possible is to ask what are the conditions which make synthetic *a priori* judgements possible. For these are the kind of judgements which characterise science. As synthetic, such judgements genuinely augment or amplify the concept of the subject and thus are more than mere tautologies. As *a priori*, they express necessity and strict universality, i.e. they transcend the contingency and particularity of sheer experience. In science what we seek is precisely such ampliative knowledge enjoying the properties of necessity and universality.

Kant insists that we have no way of vindicating the possibility of such knowledge—a possibility effectively actualised in physics and mathematics—if we persist in the traditional view that knowledge consists fundamentally in a conformity of the mind to given objects of experience. For Hume has clearly shown that from sheer experience one cannot extract the necessity and universality appropriate to scientific knowledge. The transition from the 'in fact' and the 'some' of experience to the 'necessarily' and the 'all' of science cannot be justified if knowledge is taken to be essentially a passive conformity of the mind to objects given in experience. To resolve this difficulty Kant proposed a revolutionary new way of envisaging the cognitional situation which has had considerable repercussions on the question of our knowledge of God.

He proposed that instead of considering knowledge as a conformity of mind to the given structure of objects we consider it rather as a conformity of objects to the structure of the mind.[2] According to this conception the raw material of knowledge, the given of sense experience, is *transformed* into intelligible reality by the activity of our minds. It is intuited under the *a priori* forms of space and time and understood through the application of various *a priori* categories of the understanding such as causality, subsistence, reciprocity etc. If nature presents itself as amenable to empirical investigation which yields scientific knowledge, this is because the 'nature' which we investigate is not some absolute order of things as they are in themselves independently of our knowledge of them. It is rather an ordered world of experience which is ordered precisely by being unified, assembled and 'com-prehended' in accordance with the general features of our human sensibility and understanding. In Kant's own words: 'the order and regularity in the appearances, which we entitle *nature,* we ourselves introduce. We could never find them in appearances, had not we ourselves, or the nature of our mind, set them there.'[3] All scientific knowledge of reality derives from and resides within the unified context of two indispensable and co-ordinate poles—the intuited data of sensible experience and the categories of the understanding whose role in affording knowledge of reality is confined to making these data of experience meaningful.

> Knowledge involves two factors: first, the concept, through which an object in general is thought (the category); and secondly, the intuition, through which it is given. . . . Now, the only intuition possible to us is sensible; consequently, the thought of an object in general, by means of a pure concept of understanding, can become knowledge for us only in so far as the concept is related to objects of the senses. . . .Our conclusion is therefore this: the categories, as yielding knowledge of things, have no kind of application, save only in regard to things which may be objects of possible experience.[4]

From even this very brief indication of Kant's general epistemological position one can discern how it contains the seeds of his subsequent repudiation of the claim of traditional metaphysics to provide scientific knowledge of the existence of God. Stated in its simplest terms his objection would be that God, whose existence is alleged to be necessarily or scientifically established, is not given as a datum of sensible intuition and is therefore quite beyond the scope of scientific verification. For the categories, such as causality, through which we do in fact arrive at scientific knowledge are categories whose function is precisely and exclusively to organise that which is or can be a datum of sensible intuition. Thus, since only what can be given in sense experience may be characterised legitimately as a cause, to affirm the existence of God as the first cause of the whole world is illegitimate because neither God nor the whole world could be objects of sense experience.[5]

According to Kant the traditional objects of 'special' metaphysics, namely, 'the world', 'the soul' and 'God' are not to be understood as ontological realities of which we can have theoretical scientific knowledge. He calls them transcendental ideas of pure reason. They are not applicable to the data of sense experience. Nor have we any intellectual intuition of objects corresponding to them. Their role is a simply regulative one of promoting the systematic unification of the empirical cognitions of the understanding. 'Just as the understanding unifies the manifold in the object by means of concepts, so reason unifies the manifold of concepts by means of ideas, positing a certain collective unity as the goal of the activities of the understanding, which otherwise are concerned solely with distributive unity. I accordingly maintain that transcendental ideas never allow of any constitutive employment. When regarded in that mistaken manner, and therefore as supplying concepts of certain objects, they are but pseudo-rational, merely dialectical concepts.'⁶ Properly understood, the transcendental ideas will be considered as purely normative. They will be considered as simply providing a basic heuristic structure or abiding ideal of complete rational unification which animates the endlessly ongoing investigations of natural science. In other words, the mind in its quest for scientific understanding of the given of experience proceeds as though ideally the manifold of sense experience constituted an indefinitely articulated causal system which discloses itself to a substantial spiritual ego and which depends upon on all-embracing plenitude of intelligibility and being. Traditional metaphysics has reified this merely normative ideal of meaningfulness and has considered the world, the soul and God to be real *objects* of scientific interest. It overlooks the fact that only what can be given in experience may be a real object of scientific knowledge and that the world, the soul and God can never be so given.

Kant fully appreciated the far-reaching consequences of his contention that the idea of God as wise and omnipotent

Author of the world is simply a rational strategy through which we pursue the greatest possible systematic and purposive unification of our empirical knowledge. In effect the view proposed by Kant proclaimed that what was hitherto held to be the most sublime form of human knowledge, namely the knowledge of God achieved in speculative metaphysics, was sheer illusion, and indeed dangerous illusion. Such speculation, he argued, involved one in fruitless and acrimonious disputes about what, in principle, could never be an object of genuine knowledge. It also undermined our truly scientific research into the intrinsic laws of nature by tending to substitute deceptive *deus ex machina* final solutions for the never-ending painstaking task of the empirical investigation of nature. Thus in Kant's estimation traditional metaphysical speculation about the existence of God is a source of mystification which alienates us from our true goal of establishing ourselves more effectively within the finite world. It is based on an uncritical acceptance of simply regulative ideas as constitutive sources of transcendent knowledge. It thereby gives rise 'by a dazzling and deceptive illusion, to persuasion and a merely fictitious knowledge, and therewith to contradictions and eternal disputes.'[7]

He elaborates this general philosophical position, which precludes any metaphysical proof of God's existence, by advancing a specific critique of traditional proofs for the existence of God. According to him, any such proof worthy of consideration will be an instance of one of three possible kinds of proof. These are: 1) the ontological proof; 2) the cosmological proof; 3) the physico-theological proof. They differ in that the first abstracts from all experience, the second is based on the experience of existence in general, and the third is based on the distinctive character of the world of sensible experience. Kant examines each of these possible proofs in turn.

He explains the ontological proof as the attempt to argue directly from the concept of God to his actual existence. God conceived as the infinitely perfect being who possesses all reality is judged to exist because this concept of God as *ens realissimum* is seen, on reflection, to include the property of existence just as surely as the concept of triangle is seen to include the property of having three angles. Hence from the idea itself of God we can pass at once to the affirmation of His necessary existence.

According to Kant, this proof is defective on many counts. One way of appreciating this is to consider whether the proposition which purports to confirm the existence of God, namely 'the *ens realissimum* exists', is analytic or synthetic. If it is analytic then the argument is no more than a miserable tautology which assumes the existence of an *ens realissimum* and then merely asserts the existence thus assumed. If, as is indeed the case, the proposition is synthetic then it cannot be contradictory to deny the existence of the envisaged *ens realissimum,* since only of analytic propositions is it contradictory to affirm the subject and deny the predicate. It is a feature of synthetic propositions that the concept of the predicate is not contained within the concept of the subject and that, therefore, it can be denied without contradiction.

More fundamentally, the error of the proof resides in its mistaken contention that existence is a further determining characteristic of our concept of a thing which can function as a genuine predicate of this concept. The truth of the matter is that when we say that something exists we do not announce a new predicate but merely posit the subject and all its predicates as an object which corresponds to our concept of it. Consequently, from our idea of God, however much we embellish it with connotations of absolute and unlimited perfection, we cannot arrive directly at any conclusion concerning the existence of an object corresponding to this idea. At most we can say that our concept of God as *ens realissimum* is not evidently incompatible with actual existence. However, the question still remains whether or not such a being really exists. As Kant himself puts it: 'When, therefore, I think a being as the supreme reality, without any defect, the question still remains whether it exists or not.'[8] We can have no knowledge of the answer to this question because we can only confirm the existence of objects that can be given in experience, and God is not that kind of object.

Kant suggests that at first sight the cosmological proof appears more promising than the ontological. Its point of departure is not an idea but rather real experience, namely, the experience of contingent existence. It argues from the experience of contingent beings to the existence of God as the absolutely necessary cause of everything contingent. However, in Kant's estimation, this argument is only superficially more plausible than the ontological proof. On closer examination each of its two main steps is seen to involve discrediting fallacies. These two steps are: 1) the causal argument to the existence of an absolutely necessary being; 2) the identification of this absolutely necessary being with God conceived as *ens realissimum*.

The chief objection to the first step is that it misuses the principle of causality by employing it to advance beyond its legitimate use within the world of contingent sensible experience to the existence of a necessary being as the transcendent cause of the whole order of contingent beings. This misuse of causality arises from an unwarranted transformation of a regulative principle of thought into a constitutive one. In other words, a rational exigency—in accordance with which we must unremittingly explore the domain of contingent beings as though in quest of a never empirically given, necessary ground of this domain—is transformed into an assertion of the independent objective existence of this heuristic ideal.

However, even if one accepted the argument from the experience of contingent beings to the existence of a necessary being, one would still be confronted with difficulties in the second step of the proof which identifies this necessary being with God. In Kant's estimation this step reintroduces a concealed version of the ontological argument. In seeking to determine the empirically indeterminate notion of an

c

absolutely necessary being it appeals to the *a priori* concept of *ens realissimum* as the only one which can adequately express what is meant by this notion. But this is equivalent to asserting that from the concept of *ens realissimum* one can infer that of absolutely necessary being, which is precisely the ontological argument. Kant lays out this final critique of the cosmological proof in logical form as follows:

> If the proposition, that every absolutely necessary being is likewise the most real of all beings, is correct (and this is the *nervus probandi* of the cosmological proof), it must, like all affirmative judgements, be convertible, at least *per accidens*. It therefore follows that some *entia realissima* are likewise absolutely necessary beings. But one *ens realissimum* is in no respect different from another, and what is true of *some* under this concept is true also of *all*. In this case, therefore, I can convert the proposition *simpliciter,* not only *per accidens,* and say that every *ens realissimum* is a necessary being. But since this proposition is determined from its *a priori* concepts alone, the mere concept of the *ens realissimum* must carry with it the absolute necessity of that being: and this is precisely what the ontological proof has asserted and what the cosmological proof has refused to admit, although the conclusions of the latter are indeed covertly based on it.[9]

Turning, finally, to the physico-theological proof Kant observes that it should be treated with respect and admits that at the common-sense level of thought it strengthens belief in God. He insists, however, that at the level of critical philosophical discussion it is no more intellectually compelling than the other two proofs already considered. He describes the physico-theological proof as one which argues from the order, purposiveness and beauty which pertain to things contingently throughout the world of our experience to their absolute origin in an intelligent cause which is envisaged as a supremely perfect being. He admits that there is a certain plausibility in arguing analogically from artifacts such as houses and watches implying an intelligent cause to the harmonious products and processes of nature likewise implying an intelligent cause. But he contends that even if this line of thought were accepted it would entitle us merely to affirm the existence of a finite intelligent *architect* of the form of the world who is limited by the adaptability of the material in which he works. It would not establish that the divine architect must be a supremely perfect being who is the *creator* of the matter as well as the form of the world. In leading us only to the point of admiring the indeterminate greatness, wisdom and power of the author of the world, and not to the affirmation of a supreme omnipotent creator, the physico-theological approach fails to attain a divine reality which could form the basis of theology and religion.

In order to bridge this gap between finite architect and supreme creator the physico-theological argument abandons all specific empirical considerations and falls back upon the cosmological proof. In other words it has recourse to the *contingency* of the purposive order of the world, and from this contingency alone it advances to affirm the existence of an absolutely necessary being. In the cosmological proof this absolutely necessary being is ultimately identified with God envisaged as an all-embracing supreme reality. We have already seen how, for Kant, this ultimate step of the cosmological proof depends upon an appeal to the ontological proof. Thus the physico-theological proof collapses into the cosmological proof, which in turn collapses into the ontological proof, which is itself patently invalid. Hence, in Kant's estimation, since these are the only three possible kinds of argument, any attempt to provide a speculative proof for the existence of God along the lines of traditional metaphysics is demonstrated to be impossible.

Kant's critique of the proofs for God has exercised a profound influence upon subsequent thought and contributed significantly to the formation of contemporary philosophical atheism. Even today it is widely and often uncritically accepted that he has definitively demolished the possibility of a rational proof for God in the traditional sense of the term. In the course of this study we shall have several occasions to refer to this aspect of Kant's thought. However, his contribution to the problem of God, and to the development of atheism, is not confined to this topic. In order to arrive at a judicious appraisal of his far-reaching significance it is important to understand why, and in what sense, he himself did not consider his total philosophical position to be atheistic but, on the contrary, a defence of the possibility of a particular form of religious belief.

Immediately after his critique of the proofs for God, Kant explicitly warns us against jumping to atheistic conclusions. He points out that the self-same grounds which preclude a metaphysical demonstration of the existence of God likewise preclude the validity of all counter-assertions. What is sauce for the goose is sauce for the gander and if we cannot validly speculate beyond experience to the existence of a supreme being as the ultimate ground of all things, by the same token we cannot speculate beyond experience to the non-existence of this supreme being.

Moreover, in Kant's view, the work of speculative theology is not entirely without value in respect of our knowledge of God. For if by some other means than speculative theology we have reason to affirm the existence of a supreme being then the reflections of speculative theology on the idea of God will serve a most useful function in purifying and enriching our understanding of this being. In effect, he upholds a definite role for speculative theology by viewing it as a refinement of a basic moral and religious conviction rather than as a basis of such conviction.

Thus, while for the merely speculative employment of reason the supreme being remains a mere *ideal*, it is yet *an ideal without a flaw*, a concept which completes and crowns the whole of human knowledge. Its objective reality cannot indeed be proved, but also cannot be disproved, by merely speculative reason. If, then, there should be a moral theology that can make good this deficiency, transcendental theology, which before was problematic only, will prove itself indispensable in determining the concept of this supreme being and in constantly testing reason, which is so often deceived by sensibility, and which is frequently out of harmony with its own ideas.[10]

A benign interpretation of Kant, from a theistic viewpoint, is one which suggests that the aim even of his critique of the proofs for God is not to inculcate complete theoretical agnosticism but rather to pave the way for a more authentic affirmation of God.[11] Thus, having restricted (perhaps somewhat arbitrarily and too exclusively) the meaning of 'knowledge' to the scientific understanding of phenomenal objects and their laws, in denying that we can have theoretical knowledge of the existence of God, he was merely denying that God can be known after the manner of a physical object. Since God is in no sense a component of the physical world he cannot, strictly speaking, be affirmed as an object of theoretical knowledge. If he is to be affirmed it will not be through the medium of scientific knowledge but rather through a form of affirmation which transcends scientific knowledge and which, for want of a better term, might be called rational faith. Thus when referring to the problem of God in the Preface to the second edition of the *Critique of Pure Reason* Kant observes: 'I have therefore found it necessary to deny knowledge, in order to make room for faith.'[12]

Prescinding from a discussion of whether this benign interpretation is adequate to the sweeping and uncompromising character of Kant's critique of the proofs, let us consider in what sense there is room in his thought for a stable affirmation of God through rational faith. Since such an affirmation finds no place in Kant's account of the authentic rationality of theoretical knowledge, it must, if it is to be sustained at all, pertain to the rationality of practical knowledge. It is here through reflection upon reason in its moral use that he achieves an affirmation of the existence of God. His existence is affirmed as a postulate or presupposition of morality.[13]

It is important to understand that when Kant speaks of God as a postulate of morality, he does not at all mean that belief in God is the basis or motivating principle of morality. Indeed, as has been mentioned earlier, one of the decisive features of Kant's contribution to the new humanism of liberty is his insistence upon the autonomy of morality. He points out that:

> So far as morality is based upon the conception of man as a free agent who, just because he is free, binds himself through his reason to unconditioned laws, it stands in need neither of the idea of another Being over him, for him to apprehend his duty, nor of an incentive other than the law itself, for him to do his duty. At least it is man's own fault if he is subject to such a need; and if he is, this need can be relieved through nothing outside himself: for whatever does not originate in himself and in his own freedom in no way compensates for the deficiency of his morality. Hence for its own sake morality does not need religion at all (whether objectively, as regards willing, or subjectively, as regards ability [to act]); by virtue of pure practical reason it is self-sufficient.[14]

The existence of God is postulated in the context of practical reason not as the foundation of morality but as a condition of the due fulfilment of its rational exigencies. The moral law, which man through his practical reason imposes upon himself, directs him to seek an unconditioned object; the *summum bonum* or highest good. Upon reflection this object is seen to be a complex one. In the first place it involves the supreme unconditioned condition of all moral action, namely, a dutiful will or virtue. But over and above this necessary but insufficient condition of the *summum bonum* there is a further component, namely, the enjoyment of happiness in due proportion to virtue. The affirmation of God is required in order to render possible and to assure the necessary bond between these two components of the *summum bonum*. Let us see why this is so.

Although the pursuit of happiness cannot be the criterion of moral action nevertheless to act morally or virtuously is to behave in such a manner as to be worthy or deserving of happiness. He who so behaves should be able to hope for and expect happiness. No rational appraisal of how things should be, could decide otherwise. 'For to need happiness, to deserve it, and yet at the same time not to participate in it, cannot be consistent with the perfect volition of a rational being.'[15] But the ultimate coherence of this rational exigency or practical necessity that virtue should produce due happiness and thus accomplish the whole or perfect good, which the moral law bids us to promote, requires that God should exist. Happiness depends upon the harmony of the course of nature with a man's wish and will. Since the human will cannot dictate the course of natural events, the necessary connexion between virtue and happiness can be assured only through recourse to an infinite being, who alone can guarantee the ultimate accomplishment of a state of affairs in which happiness is exactly proportioned to virtue. In other words, since we recognise that it is a duty to promote the *summum bonum* and must therefore presuppose its possibility, and since it is possible only on the condition of the existence of God, it is therefore morally necessary to affirm the existence of God.[16]

Thus the existence of God is affirmed by Kant, not as a speculative truth to resolve a metaphysical contradiction, but rather as an existential truth to resolve a lived conflict and disproportion in the ethical man between empirical happiness and fidelity to the demands of duty. Given that a life governed by reverence for the sacredness of dutiful behaviour is not inevitably accompanied in experience by the happiness which is appropriate and due to such a virtuous life, man in response to a rational demand for hope affirms the existence of an infinite God, who can in the fullness of time effect a total reconciliation between virtue and happiness. 'Admitting that the pure moral law inexorably binds every man as a command (not as a rule of prudence), the righteous man may say: I *will* that there be a God, that my existence in this world be also an existence outside the chain of physical causes, and in a pure world of the understanding, and lastly, that my duration be endless.'[17]

The trans-speculative and decidedly existential character of Kant's affirmation of God is highlighted by his insistence that it is inappropriate to impose the impersonal mode of discourse upon a statement of theistic certainty. The latter is essentially personal since it is out of a concrete reflection upon my own subjectivity in its moral dimension that I draw my theistic conviction. Thus he observes: 'my conviction is not *logical,* but *moral* certainty; and since it rests on subjective grounds (of the moral sentiment), I must not even say, "*It is* morally certain that there is a God, etc.", but "*I am* morally certain, etc."* In other words, belief in a God and in another world is so interwoven with my moral sentiment that as there is little danger of my losing the latter, there is equally little cause for fear that the former can ever be taken from me.'[18]

Kant's restriction of an affirmation of God to the context of practical reason has important and far-reaching consequences in his discussion of religion which we must now briefly consider. The basic work in which his philosophy of religion finds expression is his *Religion within the Limits of Reason alone* (1793). The title itself is a clear indication of his fundamental conviction that the philosophical critique of knowledge and morality is the absolute standard in terms of which any claims of religion must be regulated and judged. His reflections upon the exigencies of practical reason, which enabled him to transcend the illusions of speculative natural theology in the direction of an affirmation of God, prove to be a two-edged sword. For they lead him to repudiate the idea of supernatural revelation and to subordinate Christian faith to moral philosophy.[19]

Kant's insistence that morality arises only from a rational will's obedience to *self-imposed* universal laws, and his determination not to compromise this crowning glory of man, his moral autonomy, colours his whole attitude to religion. He admits that morality certainly leads us to religion and to the affirmation of God as supreme Lawgiver. Religion is the recognition of all duties as divine commands. But it would be a perversion of both man and religion to argue that I must know in advance that something is a divine command in order to recognise it as my duty, or to suppose that there could be a revealed religion which is so constituted that it comprises more than men could and ought to have discovered themselves merely through the use of their own reason.[20] For Kant the rational exigencies of man's practical reason constitute the fundamental and exclusive measure of true religion and the only safeguard against superstition and idolatry. 'Though it does indeed sound dangerous, it is in no way reprehensible to say that every man *creates a God* for himself, nay, must make himself such a God according to moral concepts . . . in order to honour in Him *the One who created him*.'[21]

Not only is God to be conceived through moral concepts but also religion itself must take a practical moral form. 'The one true religion comprises nothing but laws, that is, those practical principles of whose unconditioned necessity we can become aware, and which we therefore recognise as revealed through pure reason (not empirically).'[22] The true veneration of God the supreme Lawgiver consists simply in living a good moral life. We should of course cultivate a sense of the presence and holiness of God but this is to be done in the context of moral behaviour, not in isolation. Thus Kant observes: 'I take the following proposition to be a principle requiring no proof: *Whatever, over and above good-life conduct,*

*man fancies that he can do to become well-pleasing to God is mere
religious illusion and pseudo-service of God.'*[23]

Kant's rationalistic and moralistic conception of religion
convinced him that in its traditional credal forms religion is
a form of self-deception and alienation. Although he did
indeed count himself a Christian his interpretation of
Christianity is one which envisages Christ as a teacher of a
purely moral religion—the religion of pure practical
reason.[24] He rejected worship, prayer and all religious
practices directed exclusively to the service of God as merely
the trappings of a 'fetish-faith'. He saw them as tending to
substitute evasive other-worldly illusions of righteousness for
the more demanding but authentic requirements of this-
worldly moral behaviour.[25] Even more objectionable, in his
estimation, is any suggestion that faith in supernatural
revelation is itself a source of justification. This could only
express a craven abdication of one's personal autonomy and
rational integrity.

The notion that *belief* in such a revelation, as the sacred
history recounts it to us, and *acknowledgement* of it (whether
inwardly or outwardly) are in themselves means whereby
we render ourselves well-pleasing to God, would be a
dangerous religious illusion. For this belief, as an inner
confession of his steadfast conviction, is so genuinely an
action which is compelled by fear that an upright man
might agree to any other condition sooner than to this;
for in the case of all other compulsory services he would at
most be doing something merely superfluous, whereas here,
in a declaration, of whose truth he is not convinced, he
would be doing violence to his conscience.[26]

Kant's philosophy of religion has been aptly described as
anthropocentric not theocentric. Although retaining the
affirmation of a God endowed with most of the properties
ascribed to him in traditional natural theology, the whole
context of this affirmation is profoundly modified. The

affirmation is not in the service of a better understanding of divine revelation or even of an ultimate understanding of man's meaning and value elaborated in terms of its transcendent theistic foundation. Instead the Cartesian swing to subjectivity, inflected in the direction of practical reason, has begun to unfold its inherent immanentistic logic. The fundamental and irreducible perspective of Kant's thought which provides the enveloping context within which everything must be ordered is the autonomy of man's pure practical reason. This autonomy or power to produce moral decisions in accordance with a law which proceeds from practical reason itself is the fundamental fact which must govern our appraisal of everything else. A religious affirmation of God is indeed required by the exigencies of pure practical reason but the scope of this affirmation must also be rigidly controlled within the limits of these requirements under pain of compromising our moral autonomy. This and other aspects of Kant's thought which we have noted have had a considerable bearing upon the subsequent course of philosophy of religion in general and upon the evolution of contemporary atheism in particular. Let us mention some of the more influential features of his total viewpoint.

The epistemological position developed by Kant in the *Critique of Pure Reason,* although claiming to leave the existence of God an open question, lends itself readily, particularly if considered in isolation from his other works, to an intrinsically atheistic outlook. Its positive insistence that scientific knowledge of God's existence is not accessible to the methods of physical science appears less philosophically innocuous when seen in the light of the further assertion that the *only* scientific knowledge of objective existence is that afforded by physical science. If God cannot be known in the way in which positive science makes things known, and if the latter is the only way in which something can be *really known,* then a subsequent philosophical position which, admittedly unlike Kant's, gives absolute priority to such theoretical considerations will have no reason to affirm the existence of God. In this way, as we shall see, Kant's theory of knowledge has proved to be a fertile source of inspiration to various forms of atheistic naturalism and positivism.

This consequence has been reinforced by the remarkable impact of Kant's critique of the proofs for God. It has been widely supposed that this critique constitutes Kant's final word on the question of God's existence. Likewise it has been supposed that the critique has discredited all possible forms of proof for God and that its validity is independent even of Kant's particular theory of knowledge. Thus, as one contemporary philosopher accurately remarks, 'It is not, in fact, very common for secular philosophers nowadays even to advance reasons for not considering arguments for the existence of God. Perhaps this is because Kant is credited with having done so once for all.'[27] The cumulative psychological effect of these questionable suppositions has been a tendency to interpret all traditional proofs for God in Kantian terms and to deflect interest away from the theme of demonstrating God's existence as in principle a hopeless project.

On the other hand Kant's substitution of existential and practical considerations for an objective theoretical approach to God has encouraged in different ways various attempts to abandon or surpass the ideal of scientific detachment in this domain. One detects this influence, in a somewhat debased form, in the late eighteenth-century and early nineteenth-century writings of thinkers such as Schleiermacher, Jacobi, Schelling and even the young Hegel. In such writings the affirmation of a quasi-intuitive awareness of the divine reality, by claiming too much too easily, tended ultimately to discredit and nullify the meaningfulness of any affirmation of God.

It is also worth noting that the practical dilemma of the lived disproportion between virtue and happiness upon which Kant based his affirmation of God has been seen in a very different light by many writers. For example, even thinkers as disparate as Marx and Camus both indignantly reject any appeal to God to resolve the phenomenon of unmerited human misery as an unworthy and ineffectual exercise in escapism. In a similar fashion, as we shall see in more detail presently, Kant's notion of 'rational faith' in the existence of God has exercised an ambiguous influence in subsequent philosophical discussion. Thus although enjoying some favour in certain versions of existentialism, in other versions, such as those of Sartre and Jeanson, it is transformed into a 'rational faith' in the non-existence of God.[28]

Perhaps the most consequential feature of Kant's thought is one to which we have already alluded, namely, its decidedly anthropocentric and this-worldly character. In its basic inspiration it tends to deflect the quest for the source of meaning and value away from a divinely ordered and ordained plan of things and to direct it rather towards the productive resources of human subjectivity. The intelligible and ethical dimensions of the world as it is described by Kant resemble more an emanation of the human spirit than a participation in divine perfection. Moreover, the basic role of both theoretical and practical endeavour is to establish us more authentically within the finite world rather than to expose us to the contemplation and imitation of things divine. Transcendence no longer refers primarily to the boundless perfection in virtue of which God is utterly beyond His created world. It refers rather to the intrinsic resources of *our* subjectivity in virtue of which *we* go beyond the sheer facticity of experience and transform it into an ordered and ethical universe. Although this outlook does allow for the affirmation of God it is inherently disposed to see this affirmation as a potential source of illusion and alienation. We have noted that instances of such alienation and illusion are detected by Kant 1) in the claims of natural theology to provide theoretical knowledge of God; 2) in the view which would make God a basis or motivating principle of morality; and 3) in the traditional beliefs and practices of revealed religion.

A question which such considerations pose is whether or not Kant's affirmation of God is really compatible with his predominantly anthropocentric viewpoint? If one grants the affirmation of God, must not the claims of this viewpoint be relativised in a manner which Kant would be unwilling to accept? In the first chapter we intimated that Descartes' ultimately theistic viewpoint radically curtailed the claims of subjectivity implicit in his doctrine of the *cogito*. One might suspect that by his emphatic insistence upon these claims Kant may, in the final analysis, have compromised the viability and coherence of his affirmation of God. This suspicion would appear to be borne out by the subsequent course of philosophical atheism which argues strenuously that a consistent anthropocentric viewpoint is incompatible with belief in a theistic conception of reality. However, before considering the explicit assertions of this view we must mention one more development which paved the way for them. This is the philosophy of Hegel which can be seen as a great metaphysical attempt to counteract the suggestion that belief in God is a source of alienation. It attempts to reconcile the anthropocentric and theocentric viewpoints, albeit at the expense of the traditional conceptions of both man and God. An outline of this remarkable attempt is the purpose of the following chapter.

3

Hegel and the Immanent Absolute

THE thought of G. W. F. Hegel (1770–1831), undoubtedly
one of the greatest philosophers of all time, is by any standard
exceptionally difficult. The great variety of interpretations
which it has inspired is evidence of its inherent complexity
and perhaps even ambiguity. It has frequently been im-
patiently dismissed as distorting the rich texture of lived
reality into a phantom maze of obscure metaphysical
tensions. The view is widespread that it is a barren system
of abstract thought whose relationship to concrete reality is
quite remote and artificial.

Although this impression is understandable in view of
Hegel's rather abstruse mode of expression it is nevertheless
quite misleading. One would be greatly mistaken in treating
Hegel as merely somebody who worked out an ingenious and
even beautiful system of ideas about an ideal world but a
system which is irrelevant to the real world of existential
concern and lived experience. For, from one point of view,
his thought can be validly considered as a dedicated quest
for the ultimate meaning and value of experience by a deeply
involved subject seeking a salvific direction for his life. It is a
sustained endeavour to resolve a crucial problem, whose
paradoxical character had been imposing itself with ever
increasing urgency in the development of modern thought,
namely, the problem of the coexistence of the finite and the
infinite. Moreover, Hegel did not raise the problem in purely

general and philosophical terms. For him the problem
presented itself first of all in his attempt to comprehend the
true significance of the object of his reverence, the Christian
religion. His early writings, such as *The Positivity of the
Christian Religion* and *The Spirit of Christianity and its Fate,* are
distinctively theological.[1] Moreover, as we shall see, in his
subsequent specifically philosophical thought these theological reflections are assimilated and transformed rather than
discarded and repudiated. The following pages comprise an
account of the broad outlines of Hegel's thought on this
problem of the coexistence of the finite and the infinite.

In his early essay *The Positivity of the Christian Religion,*
Hegel criticised the historical development of Christianity into
an authoritarian dogmatic system. His critique had a dual
inspiration. On the one hand there was his romantic
attraction to the beauty and naturalness of Greek folk
religion, which he esteemed as reflecting the harmony and
equilibrium of a truly free people. On the other hand there
was his admiration and respect for the serene rationalism of
Kant's ethical teaching. We have seen how in his *Religion
within the Limits of Reason alone* Kant had argued that the only
true worship of God consisted in fidelity to the moral imperatives of man's practical reason. Such a view commended
itself to the young Hegel who was repelled by the 'imposed',
'institutional' and 'dogmatic' character of Christianity as it
had been presented to him. Such Christianity in virtue of its
positivity could only be a source of alienation—a religion
for servile men. It was a far remove from the aim and essence
of all true religion, namely, human morality and obedience
to the moral law. This, in Hegel's opinion, was the only aim
pursued in the religious teaching of Jesus who 'undertook to
raise religion and virtue to morality and to restore to
morality the freedom which is its essence. . . . Jesus, on this
view, was the teacher of a purely moral religion, not a
positive one.'[2]

Hegel argues that because Jesus' disciples, victims of a
servile heritage, adverted primarily to the unique and

seemingly miraculous characteristics of his life they conveyed to posterity a distorted and 'positive' interpretation of the purely moral religion which Jesus wished to teach. However, in condemning positivity Hegel did not mean that genuine religious truth must be expressed only in terms of some abstract and universal concept of human nature, and without any reference to the particular historical circumstances of different cultural contexts. In the third part of his essay he dismissed such a view as an excessive rationalism which 'leaves the main problem untouched, namely, the problem of showing religion's appropriateness to nature through all nature's modifications from one century to another.'[3] Just as the living nature of an individual man necessarily involves modifications which to the mere concept of human nature are accidental superfluities, so also the content of concrete religion is always positive in the sense that it necessarily involves a contour of historical detail.

When Hegel criticises positive religion he is referring to a certain way of interpreting the significance of religion. He tells us that 'the question about positivity does not affect the content of a religion so much as the way in which the religion is conceived.'[4] Thus it is not the mere presence of historical contingencies in the teaching of a religion which constitutes its positivity but rather attributing to these contingencies, precisely as such, a supernatural significance which they do not really have. More specifically, a religion is positive when it is understood as an arbitrary and authoritarian imposition of a system of dogmas and of commands, by a radically transcendent God. On the contrary any religion, however encumbered with historical detail, can avoid the charge of positivity if it is understood as mediating to man the divine reality in the depths of his being, a reality whose vivifying power is made effective through man's free and reverent commitment to the moral law.

It is significant that even in this early phase of his thought Hegel links the question of positivity to the problem of the relation between human and divine nature, between the

D

finite and the infinite. Indeed he explicitly observes that 'an examination of this question cannot be thoughtfully and thoroughly pursued without becoming in the end a meta-physical treatment of the relation between the finite and the infinite.'[5] However, he points out that the development of such a metaphysical treatment is not the aim of this essay. His chief concern is rather to confirm his general principle 'that the aim and essence of all true religion, our religion included, is human morality, and that all the more detailed doctrines of Christianity, all means of propagating them, and all its obligations . . . have their worth and their sanctity appraised according to their close or distant connection with that aim.'[6]

In *The Spirit of Christianity and its Fate* one notes an important development in Hegel's attempt to dispel the suggestion that the Christian religion, properly considered, involves the alienation of man. Here he no longer considers it adequate merely to substitute for the positivity of tradi-tional Christianity an account of Christianity as a virtue religion embodying the Kantian doctrine of man's free consent to a self-imposed morality. In fact the influence of the Enlightenment generally gives way to a more romantic vision in which a pantheism of love rather than the moral law of practical reason is proposed as the essential message of Christianity.

In this essay the Jewish religion is criticised as effecting a radical dehumanisation of man. It is argued that in Judaism man is reduced to the condition of a slave blindly submitting to an oppressive legalism imposed by an external authority in the name of an omnipotent transcendent God. The God of the Jews is an authoritarian master and they themselves an isolated and alienated people.

According to Hegel the teaching of Jesus was intended to overcome this alienation of man. However, if such is the case, it is not very helpful to interpret this teaching along the lines of a Kantian respect for the moral law, an approach which implies a sharp distinction between duty and inclination.

For in the final analysis the Kantian doctrine of an autonomous will promulgating a universal morality is itself a type of legalism and hence a source of alienation. The master-slave relationship is merely interiorised and man as an affective living individual is dominated by man as a universal legislating reason. He is required to submit to rational commands which, in so far as his passions and inclinations are concerned, are just as imposed and positive as any positive religious commandments. Consequently, in such a view, positivity is only partially eradicated. Thus Hegel observes that 'between the Shaman of the Tungus, the European prelate who rules church and state, the Voguls, and the Puritans, on the one hand, and the man who listens to his own commands of duty, on the other, the difference is not that the former make themselves slaves while the latter is free, but that the former have their lord outside themselves, while the latter carries his lord in himself, yet at the same time is his own slave.'[7]

The true meaning of the teaching of Jesus is that a morality of laws and rules must give way to a morality of love. The Kantian moral imperative owes its quality as an imperative to a supposed enduring cleavage between duty and inclination. As a moral teaching it prides itself upon its subordination of inclination to duty. In other words it accepts as basic a dividedness within man and proposes as a moral ideal the subordination of lived inclination to life as conceptualised in the imperatives of practical reason. Reverence for the 'thou shalt' of the moral imperative is proposed as the essence of morality. Jesus repudiated as inadequate this view of the human condition. His gospel of love 'exhibits that which fulfils the law but annuls it as law and so is something higher than law and makes law superfluous.'[8] By opening our eyes to the unifying value of love Jesus overcame the alienation implicit in a morality of laws and commands. He showed that love, understood as an inner harmony of inclination and reason, is a fundamental disposition of human life, transcending the order of duties and commands. To express it in the form of an imperative is quite inadequate to its reality as a modification of life itself. If, however, we respond to an exhortation to accept the unifying power of love as the key to a truly human way of life, the *content* of the moral law will continue to be affirmed as a consequence of the logic of love. But its specifically legal *form*, its quality of legality, will have been overcome. What Jesus wished to draw to our attention was that morality must be raised from the 'thou shalt' of law to the 'is' of love. The superiority of a morality of love over one of law is illustrated by the fact that it includes the content of the latter but obviates its alienating legal form.

This moral insight has a metaphysical counterpart, namely, that the unifying power of love rather than the objectifying and analytic quality of thought is the key to the truth about reality. Through love we can come to a concrete awareness of the unity of our life with infinite life and through it with all life. 'Love itself pronounces no imperative. It is no universal opposed to a particular, no unity of the concept, but a unity of spirit, divinity. To love God is to feel one's self in the "all" of life, with no restrictions, in the infinite.'[9]

During this early period of Hegel's career he held that philosophy, envisaged as the reflective and analytic discipline *par excellence,* is incapable of achieving a rational comprehension of that loving union with infinite life which religion accomplishes. Thus in his *Fragment of a System* (1800) he affirms that philosophy is necessarily subordinate to religion. 'This partial character of the living being is transcended in religion; finite life rises to infinite life. It is only because the finite is itself life that it carries in itself the possibility of raising itself to infinite life. Philosophy therefore has to stop short of religion because it is a process of thinking and, as such a process, implies an opposition with non-thinking [processes] as well as the opposition between the thinking mind and the object of thought.'[10]

The subsequent course of Hegel's career can be considered as an attempt to work out at the level of philosophical reflection the unified conception of reality inherent in this early interpretation of Christianity as a pantheism of love. He seeks to develop a new style of philosophising which will rehabilitate reason and render accessible to it in a purified speculative form the romantic vision of reality which the gospel of Christ revealed in religious symbols. Thus whereas he might be considered a Romantic because of the longing for unity which inspired his thought he was not at all a Romantic in the manner in which he ultimately satisfied this longing. He did not rely upon vague poetical images or mystical intuitions to proclaim the profound unity of all reality. He claimed to show forth this unity as a truth adequately elaborated and fully confirmed by strictly rational procedures.[11]

Hegel's developed philosophy is a *tour de force* which seeks to overcome through rational reflection the alienating consequences of all allegedly unresolved duality.[12] The dominant theme of his philosophical maturity is that the manifold oppositions which our understanding establishes, e.g. between subject and object, mind and nature, being and thought, appearance and reality, can be reconciled dialectically by a superior philosophical rationality. In particular, he seeks to overcome, in the unity of a higher synthesis, the oppositions asserted between man and God, and between religion and philosophy. The sweep of his thought is one which envisages the transmutation of religion into an authentic form of philosophical consciousness, yielding a purely rational exposition of the ultimate unity of man and God.

This philosophical rationality takes the form of a metaphysics of spirit. In this metaphysics spirit is disclosed as the active unification of all oppositions, and all oppositions are known as ultimately reconciled self-differentiations of spirit. God, being and thought are brought into an organic unity—an onto-theo-logical synthesis—which is not simply the truth *about* reality but rather the inner living truth *of* reality. Anything less than this unified living totality would not, in Hegel's estimation, meet the exigency of radical philosophical enquiry for unity, comprehensiveness, unconditionality and autonomy. It is a unification required by the only viable philosophical first principle, namely, that the real is the rational and the rational is the real.[13]

Of particular interest, for our purposes, is Hegel's repudiation of any ultimate distinction between finite and infinite. In his view there is no serious problem concerning our knowledge of the *existence* of the infinite. It is spontaneously achieved through the religious elevation of the soul to its true principle. For religion is essentially a natural elevation of finite life to infinite life. Further, this awareness of the existence of the infinite, of which the religious impulse affords us such lively assurance, is readily confirmed by reflective appraisal. Reflection discloses that thought, in the very act of adverting to the various dimensions of finitude as such, has already transcended the barriers of finitude and attained an affirmation of the infinite as the animating source of its consciousness of finitude. As Hegel himself puts it: 'The limitation of finiteness only exists for us in so far as we are above and beyond it. . . . Thus the infinite is what is above and beyond the limits; it is something *other* than the limited; it is the unlimited, the infinite. Thus we have finite and infinite.'[14] Granted that the identity of the real and the rational is the true philosophical perspective it follows that there is no problem of a transition from the infinite as an exigency of thought to the real existence of the infinite. Similarly there is no chasm to be bridged between finite and infinite by means of causal argument. For the existence of the infinite is confirmed in the very dialectic of thought itself which discloses the rational, and thereby the real, correlativity of finite and infinite. Kant's objections to the metaphysical affirmation of the existence of the infinite are swept away as resting upon a false opposition between the real and the rational. Even the traditional 'proofs' for the existence of God of natural theology can be rehabilitated, admittedly in a modified sense, when this illusory opposition is abandoned and the true relationship of finite and infinite is appreciated. They can be accorded a certain modest role and value, not as detached impersonal demonstrations of a previously unknown infinite, but rather as descriptive elucidations of the more basic religious movement of the spirit whereby it elevates itself from finite life to infinite life. In other words 'they ought to comprise the elevation of the human spirit to God, and express it for thought'.[15]

Thus, for Hegel, the true focus of interest in a philosophical discussion of God is not so much the *existence* of the infinite as its true nature and its relationship with the finite. As one commentator puts it: 'Not the existential affirmation but the truth about the divine actuality, known to be the inclusive life of all finite modes of thought and being, is the proper purpose of the proving activity in Hegel's philosophy of God.'[16]

We must not, Hegel insists, rest complacently in a bare assertion of the infinite or be deterred by pious platitudes about the total otherness and unknowability of the infinite. 'We must rid ourselves completely of this opposition of finite and infinite, and do it by getting an insight into the real state of the case.'[17] His whole philosophy of spirit can be seen as an unrelenting effort to attain this 'insight into the real state of the case'.

In accordance with the exigency for unification which animates this whole philosophy he repudiates any ultimate opposition of finite and infinite. In contrast to the traditional causal understanding of the finite-infinite relationship, according to which the finite is totally dependent upon a self-sufficient transcendent infinite which is intrinsically and eternally independent of the freely created order of finite being, Hegel describes the order of finite being as a necessary aspect of the process whereby the infinite accomplishes its full and true reality as infinite. It accomplishes it through a process of self-differentiation and mediation whereby in finite being it negates the abstract affirmation of itself as sheer identity and thence returns to a concrete affirmation of itself through a negation of this negation. 'The finite is therefore an essential moment of the infinite in the nature of God, and thus it may be said it is God Himself who renders Himself finite, who produces determinations within Himself.'[18]

In his quest for a unified theory of reality Hegel does not succumb to any short cuts which would patently involve him in atheism by denying the reality of the infinite or in pantheistic acosmism by denying the reality of the finite. The genuine though relative reality of the finite, and the irreducible and absolute reality of the infinite must both be strenuously affirmed and their distinction must not be obliterated. What must be overcome is the tendency of pictorial religious thought and the mere abstractions of the categories of the understanding to petrify this distinction into a hard and fast and final opposition. What is required is the dialectical thinking of the philosophy of absolute spirit which discloses the *identity in distinction* between the finite and the infinite. Expressed in the form of absolute idealism this philosophy portrays the fundamental identity in distinction of finite and infinite as the necessary self-finitising process of absolute spirit through which it accomplishes its concrete universality as infinite spirit. Understood as an objectification of the divine life, the whole finite order, culminating in the religious and above all the philosophical activity of the human spirit, is seen to be required if God is to achieve that concrete knowledge of His limitless virtuality which constitutes His true infinite actuality. All the vicissitudes and alienations inherent in the finite world, and which are characteristic of this stage of 'God in His otherness', must be apprehended as necessary accompaniments of the process whereby absolute spirit returns to a realisation (in the dual sense of becoming aware and becoming real) of itself through the religious and philosophical movement of liberation of a self-transcending finite consciousness. In short, both the finite and the infinite require each other and their unity in distinction for their true reality and full intelligibility.

The following extended quotation summarises this view of Hegel concerning the relationship of finite and infinite:

For the logically developed and rational consideration of the finite, the simple forms of a proposition have no longer any value. God is infinite, I am finite; these are false, bad expressions, forms which do not adequately correspond to that which the Idea, the nature of the real object, is. The finite is not that which is, in like manner the infinite is not fixed; these determinations are only moments of the process. It is equally true that God exists as finite and the Ego as infinite. The '*is*', or exists, which is regarded in such propositions as something firmly fixed, has, when understood in its true sense, no other meaning than that of activity, vitality, and spirituality.

Nor are predicates adequate for definition here, and least of all those which are one-sided and transient. But, on the contrary, what is true, what is the Idea, exists only as movement. Thus God is this movement within Himself, and thereby alone is He the living God. But this separate existence of the finite must not be retained; it must, on the contrary, be abrogated. God is movement towards the finite, and owing to this He is, as it were, the lifting up of the finite to Himself. In the Ego, as in that which is annulling itself as finite, God returns to Himself, and only as this return is He God. Without the world God is not God.[19]

This global account of the finite-infinite relationship has considerable repercussions on many fronts. It signalises not merely the culmination and synthesis of elements of pre-Cartesian and post-Cartesian philosophical traditions but also, and more profoundly, a new departure, an *Aufhebung,* a new philosophical context which transforms the significance of the data of philosophical reflection including philosophy itself. In particular, it affects the philosophical discussion of God, religion and alienation. From the new coordinates which it establishes between these themes has emerged the framework in terms of which contemporary atheism articulates itself, and in terms of which a considerable amount of putative contemporary theism confusedly expresses itself.

If one were to designate a philosophy as theistic by reference to the ubiquity and centrality of its appeal to God then, on this criterion, Hegel's philosophy would be classified as decisively and even extravagantly theistic. Such a description would, however, be an oversimplification and potentially misleading, and has, one suspects, been at the root of much philosophical talking at cross-purposes. For it fails to take account of the profound transformation of meaning which the term 'God' undergoes in the context of Hegelian thought.

Amongst the features included within the traditional connotation of 'God' (or at least the connotation of 'God' in the philosophical mainstream of the Christian era) are those of 1) absolute freedom in respect of creation; 2) unqualified transcendence *vis-à-vis* the order of finite being; and 3) eternal immutability of perfection. Admittedly these notes reappear in the Hegelian conception of God but they do so in a highly accommodated sense.

Hegel speaks of 'the free creative activity, which can realise itself without the help of a matter that exists outside it'.[20] Similarly, he tells us: 'God creates a world, God determines; outside of Him there is nothing to determine. He determines Himself when He thinks Himself, places an Other over against Himself, when He and a world are two. God creates the world out of nothing.'[21] Thus Hegel confirms the traditional conception of divine freedom in respect of creation to the extent that he insists that God cannot be constrained to create by anything extrinsic to His nature, for other than through creation there is no being extrinsic to God. However, the traditional conception goes further and insists that God cannot be said to be constrained to create through any intrinsic necessity of nature which urges Him towards greater self-expression. For as infinite perfection He actually and eternally enjoys all the resources of being. Nor, in the traditional conception, can we attribute any necessity of creating to the divine intellect or will. The divine will cannot be said to ordain the communication of being as though realising a desirable end. On the contrary, the divine love of perfection finds complete satisfaction in His own actually infinite being. Any decision to create is adopted, not in order to achieve an unrealised perfection, but in virtue of a free choice to communicate a perfection already fully possessed.[22]

Hegel cannot subscribe to this stricter conception of divine freedom. For, in his view, the 'creation' of the finite order is an intrinsic necessity of the divine nature. It is only in virtue of the itinerary of spirit in and through the processes of finite reality that the infinite can accomplish its true reality. Only through an exteriorisation of itself in the order of finite being can the divine nature achieve the complete expression and total fulfilment of its intrinsic finality. 'Without the world God is not God.'

The meaning of divine transcendence is likewise affected in the Hegelian viewpoint. Traditionally the notion of divine transcendence has signified that God, in virtue of His infinite perfection, is really distinct from and really independent of the whole created finite order. It implies that the divine perfection is neither intrinsically modified nor limited by the reality of finite beings. It emphasises that finite and infinite are two levels of being which are strictly incommensurable. If the divine nature can be said to precontain *eminenter* the perfection of created finite realities it does so only in virtue of and in the manner of its own infinite perfection. It is in no way affected in its being by the finitude which characterises the mode of reality of created things.[23]

Hegel also affirms the transcendence of God. There is, he argues, a distinction between the infinite and the finite. The infinite perfection of the divine reality is irreducible to any given set of finite realities. However, by contrast with the traditional view, this distinction is not envisaged as though the reality of the infinite were *independent* of that of the finite. Hegel's conception of the identity in distinction of finite and infinite is one which requires that transcendence be understood as a characteristic of the divine life as operative throughout the finite order rather than as characteristic of God as radically independent of the finite order. Conversely, the realm of the finite is seen as an essential feature of the auto-constitution of the life of God.[24]

This is a conception which, in traditional terms, would be seen as attempting the impossible task of doing justice to divine transcendence in terms of the immanence of God in the finite and the participation of the finite in God but eliminating the doctrine of the self-sufficiency of God's infinite perfections *vis-à-vis* the finite. In effect, Hegel's view of transcendence signifies the dynamic 'going beyond' itself of spirit into its own otherness in the various dimensions of finitude, and the corresponding 'going beyond itself' of the finite which finally achieves the full accomplishment of absolute spirit. Thus transcendence for Hegel signifies, not a static immutable property of God, but rather a dynamic activity animating the identity in difference of finite and infinite.

Involved in his treatment of creative freedom and divine transcendence is an equivalent modification of the traditional conception of God's eternally immutable perfection. Traditionally this signified His 'simultaneous, whole and perfect possession of interminable life'. It expressed God's transcendence of time in His being and in His activity. It excluded from the divine perfection any suggestion of temporal succession or process of change.[25]

Hegel too speaks of God's eternal immutable perfection. 'The absolute, eternal Idea is, in its essential existence, in and for itself, God in His eternity before the creation of the world, and outside of the world.'[26] He is even quite lyrical on this topic telling us that 'God exists in His eternal truth, and this is thought of as the state of things which existed before time was, as the state in which God was when the blessed spirits and the morning stars, the angels, His children, sang His praises'.[27] This for him, however, is only an approximate and abstractive way of considering the divine perfection. It represents only a purely theoretical contemplation of a universal blue-print of the divine reality. 'This Universal contains the entire Idea, but it only *contains* it, it is the Idea potentially only.'[28] The concrete realisation of this potentiality implies a whole historical process of manifestation. Only through the self-finitising movement of exteriorisation and historical reflective reappropriation does the potentiality of spirit enter into adequate conscious possession of itself. 'Spirit is just this act of advance into reality by means of Nature, i.e., Spirit finds its antithesis, or opposite, in Nature, and it is by the annulling of this opposition that it exists for itself and is Spirit.'[29] Thus, notwithstanding the obvious and acute metaphysical tension between the notions of infinite eternal perfection and finite historical process the whole context of Hegel's viewpoint obliges him to bind them together in his conception of God.

These considerations illustrate what a profound transmutation the traditional understanding of 'God' has undergone in the framework of Hegel's philosophy. From a theistic viewpoint the benign interpretation of his achievement would be that, through a brilliant refinement of our philosophical understanding of the divine nature, he has vindicated for modern man an authentic affirmation of the God of Christianity.[30] In particular, it would be argued that he has reconciled the affirmation of God as the absolute source of all meaning and value with the emergent claims of human subjectivity and creativity by disclosing the fundamental identity which underlies and sustains the distinction of man and God. He showed that man and God could both be said to be the source of the meaning and value of the world because the distinction is comprehended as expressing only different dimensions of the same absolute reality.[31]

However, although such an interpretation of his philosophy of God appears to be faithful to Hegel's own intention and expressed conviction it is an inadequate account of the actual outcome of his endeavour. A more circumspect appraisal of his achievement would argue that its cumulative effect is the elimination of the affirmation of God and the substitution of an essentially non-theistic doctrine of absolute spirit. Thus, as Professor Collins justly remarks, the upshot of the new conception is to establish the truth about God and theism by elucidating their inadequacy and insensitivity to the true nature of the absolute. Hence, instead of the provisional and somewhat loose designation of his philosophy as onto-theo-logical 'the ruling framework of Hegel's philosophy is more precisely called an *onto-pneuma-logic,* to emphasise the centrality of his unique conception of self-developing spirit.'[32] This contention is reinforced by a consideration of Hegel's account of the relationship between religion and philosophy and its implications for the theme of human alienation.

Religion and philosophy are for Hegel undoubtedly the two most sublime activities of man and, more fundamentally, the two most decisive activities in the accomplishment of the full self-realisation of absolute spirit. In each of them spirit becomes consciously manifest to itself. Both of them are necessary to this process of self-manifestation which embraces the articulation of the whole of Nature and human history. But only in philosophy does this auto-constitution of spirit achieve consciousness of itself adequately and in an appropriately pure form.

For Hegel, as we have already noted, religion arises in human consciousness as a spontaneous self-transcending elevation of finite life to infinite life. This spontaneous wellspring of religion is not, however, a sheer romantic immediacy involving only sentiment, intuition, and imagination. Precisely as an activity of finite *spirit* it is a mediated immediacy involving the element of thought. It involves not just the mere feeling of dependence, which even animals who cannot transcend their limitations experience, but also a genuine cognitive transcendence of the realm of finitude mediated through concepts derived from a variety of sources, e.g. lived experience, education and revelation.[33] The true appraisal of the spontaneous pre-reflective aspect of religion and the responsive chord it strikes in human sensibility and affectivity is not that it is intransigent to rational articulation but rather that in its origin and deepest significance religion is the work of God rather than of man, the activity of absolute spirit mediated through the finite channels of human subjectivity. 'Thus religion is the Divine Spirit's knowledge of itself through the mediation of finite spirit.'[34]

Religion represents a decisive yet ambiguous phase of the life of absolute spirit. It is decisive in that it signalises the conscious self-repossession of spirit from its necessary dispersion and exteriorisation in Nature and finite cultural institutions. It is ambiguous in that although it is a true and necessary expression of spirit's conscious appropriation of itself it is not the definitive expression of this appropriation which occurs in a pure form only with the transformation of religion into philosophy. Religion, even 'the perfect religion', is inadequate to the appropriate formulation of its own content, a formulation which the philosophy of spirit alone provides.

Religion announces the conscious reconcilation of spirit with itself but the form of this announcement is coloured by overtones of the long process of alienation which has been overcome. For religion, although its object is the absolute, thinks this content in a manner characteristic of its state as intermediary between the finite realm of feeling and perception on the one hand and the liberated pure speculation of philosophy on the other. It thinks its content in the form of representational thought (*Vorstellung*).[35] This is a form of thought suspended between the particularity of imagery and the universality of rational thought. It seeks to attain to the pure universal significance intimated in a limited individual image of the absolute but fails to extricate itself effectively from the image's sensuous and 'natural' acceptation. It arrives merely at a circumscribed anticipatory representation of the absolute. According to Hegel, in considering the teachings of the various religions we must bear in mind that they express themselves in the form of representational thought. Thus, for example, the theme of the Father begetting the Son, the Creation story, the account of Christ's birth, death, and resurrection, all belong to the realm of representational thought whose truth in a pure form is accessible only to philosophy.

Although religion 'intends' the living conscious reconciliation of finite and infinite, its roots in sensibility and the concomitant limitation of its own representational form of thought expose it to the danger of misrepresenting in various ways the true relationship of finite and infinite. It is prone, for example, to represent the poles of the relationship in such exaggerated opposition that the only conscious bond which can be claimed between them is the 'unhappy consciousness' of a master-slave relationship.[36] Moreover, even when the fundamental unity in distinction of finite and infinite life finds true religious expression in the doctrines of Christianity this truth remains inadequately disclosed. For it is represented in the form of external relations and contingent events; not in the strictly rational form of 'inner connection and absolute necessity' in which the complete liberation of spirit is finally attained. 'The witness of the Spirit in its highest form takes the form of philosophy, according to which the Notion, purely as such, and without the presence of any presupposition, develops the truth out of itself, and we recognise it as developing, and perceive the necessity of the development in and through the development itself.'[37]

Thus by reference to his own philosophy of spirit taken as

an absolute standard of integral and liberated consciousness, Hegel establishes a critical relativisation of religion and a criterion which enables him to discern evidence of human alienation in different historical forms of positive religion. Hence the intimation in his early theological writings that the theme of religious positivity 'cannot be thoughtfully and thoroughly pursued without becoming in the end a metaphysical treatment of the relation between the finite and the infinite' is more than fully borne out. Not merely positivity, but also in contrast with his earlier view, religion as such is subordinated to and assimilated within the superior rationality of the philosophical system.

We cannot enter here in detail into Hegel's extremely interesting analysis of various particular religions in terms of their representation of God and man. Nor can we discuss his account of the logical progression towards genuine spiritual liberation which is accomplished through the temporal sequence of particular religions. However, as might be expected, he detects a very profound level of alienation in the forms of religion which, unlike his own conception of absolute spirit, attach particular importance to proclaiming the unqualified transcendence of God *vis-à-vis* the finite order. This is clearly illustrated in his treatment of the Jewish religion.

As described by Hegel, Judaism is the religion *par excellence* of divine transcendence.[38] It avers that God is the unique almighty Lord and that the created world is totally dependent upon His incomprehensible sublime majesty. The fundamental relationship between man and God is that of worthless slave to absolute master. God created all men for His own honour and glory. In practice, however, it is only through a divinely chosen and hence isolated people, the Jews, that this goal is to be achieved. Effectively, He is the God of Abraham, of Isaac and of Jacob.

According to this view of Jewish belief, the prerequisite of man's control of Nature, of his empirical happiness and of his attainment of the Promised Land, is acknowledgement

E

of God's absolute creative sovereignty over Nature and
human life; an acknowledgement which must be endorsed
by unquestioning submission to the divine law precisely as
such. The entire sphere of a true believer's actions must be
regulated in the most minute detail in accordance with laws
which are accepted and obeyed, not as arising from human
reason, but as handed down by God. 'The people of God
is accordingly a people adopted by covenant and contract
on the conditions of fear and service.'[39]

Thus, for Hegel, the Jew is a slave who has alienated,
handed over to God, his freedom, his autonomy, his authentic creativity and subjectivity. More precisely, he has not
yet achieved a conscious realisation of his kinship and unity
as spirit with the absolute, and of the exigencies of this
spirituality which must be satisfied in any allegedly authentic
religious relationship.[40] Because of his impoverished conception of human life he submits to an absolute dichotomy
between man and God and locates the source of any meaning
and value which might adorn human existence in the in-
scrutable providence of an utterly transcendent Lord.

The anguish and alienation inherent in the Jewish
religion prepare the way for Christianity which is, in principle, the authentic religious expression of the unity of finite
and infinite. The enslaving irreducible transcendence of God
is overcome in its doctrines of the Son of God's incarnation,
death and resurrection and the indwelling of the Spirit in
the Church. The truth herein expressed is of course obscured
by the limitation of the religious mode of representation and
must be elucidated in the light of its properly philosophical
formulation. Nevertheless, what it does express, however
imperfectly, is the necessary truth that 'the unity of the
divine and human natures has been brought into human
consciousness and has become a certainty for it, implying
that the otherness, or as it is also expressed, the finitude,
the weakness, the frailty of human nature is not incompatible with this unity, just as in the eternal Idea otherness in
no way detracts from the unity which God is.'[41]

Further, the consciousness of God as finitised in human nature, depicted in the doctrine of the Incarnation, is developed in the doctrine of Christ's passion and death into a consciousness of the abolition of this self-effacing God.[42] But consciousness is rescued from this 'the most frightful of all thoughts' that God has died, by the doctrine of the Resurrection which signalises the perfect accomplishment of the absolute as totally reconciling infinite spirit. We are brought to the liberating realisation that if we wish to speak of God we must understand Him not as the abstract transcendent God of theism but as the absolute which endures self-estrangement, finitude and even death itself in order to attain His true spiritual reality as universal self-consciousness.[43]

With our appreciation that the new conception of divine life as active encompassing resolution of all oppositions concerns not Christ alone but all humanity, we enter fully into the Kingdom of Spirit. We overcome our particularity and, notwithstanding our frailty and finitude, comprehend ourselves as part of a divine movement of reconciliation in which we are united with God and our fellow men. This new awareness finds expression in a spiritual community which in religious representation we call the Church. In this community, animated by the consciousness of our identity with the divine spiritual totality, we are, in principle, united through universal love with all men and ultimately with every dimension of our worldly existence—e.g. economic, scientific, aesthetic and political. Above all it is in its political life that the spiritual community gives most effective external witness to the liberating consciousness which animates it. 'The true reconciliation whereby the Divine realises itself in the region of reality is found in moral and legal life in the State.'[44]

Hegel attaches considerable importance to this close relationship between the spiritual liberation attained through true religion and the attainment of genuine socio-political emancipation. A social order which is estranged, irrational and devoid of freedom will certainly tend to pervert man's quest for union with God into an alienated form of religious belief. More fundamentally, however, until we have attained a truly liberating form of religious consciousness there is no possibility of an integrated social order. For 'the definite character of justice and morality has its ultimate verification for a people only in the form of an actually existing religion, and if this last is not essentially in harmony with the principles of freedom, there is always present a rent, an unresolved division or dualism.'[45]

The individual who has attained an authentic religious appreciation of the infinite worth of every man as a citizen of the Kingdom of Spirit has transcended all distinctions of authority, power, position and race. He has a basic insight into the equality of all men and has ascertained the genuine possibility and basis of an order of universal Right and a realisation of freedom.[46] But an alienated form of religious belief, which fails to convey that man's freedom is something essentially self-possessed as an intrinsic moment of the divine life rather than something set over against and dominated by a transcendent divine Will, must inevitably engender multiform alienation throughout the whole range of social and cultural life.

Everything essentially depends here on the conception of freedom which a people bears in its own self-consciousness, for in the State the conception of freedom is realised, and to this realisation the consciousness of freedom which exists in its own right essentially belongs. Such nations as do not know that man is free in his own right, live in a condition of torpor, both as regards their form of government and their religion. There is but one conception of freedom in religion and the State. This one conception is man's highest possession, and it is realised by man. A nation which has a false or bad conception of God, has also a bad State, bad government, bad laws.[47]

Having indicated how, for Hegel, Christianity is the liberating religious embodiment of the true relationship of finite and infinite, it only remains to recall once more his insistence that this relationship finds fully adequate expression only in its appropriate *philosophical* formulation. Moreover, philosophy is not merely an attempt to develop from within an encompassing Christian faith its inherent rationality but rather the supreme and comprehensive arbiter of all rationality including that of Christian faith. Although Hegel acknowledges an intimate relationship between the truth of Christianity and the truth of his philosophy of spirit, and even acknowledges the Christian religion as a necessary precondition of his philosophy, in the final analysis it is in virtue of the truth of the latter that the former is judged to be true. The truth of Christianity as absolute religion rests upon the identity of its content, portrayed in the inferior representational form of contingent historical facts and events, with the content of the philosophy of spirit, where it is articulated in its appropriate form of rational necessity. In philosophy we rise above the essentially receptive and representational form of religious faith to the absolute or divine viewpoint of speculative thought which re-enacts the rational necessity of the whole process of spirit's self-othering and self-reconciliation. From this divine perspective of philosophic thought the life of religious faith is surpassed and comprehended as the penultimate stage in the accomplishment of divine self-knowledge.

Admittedly the generality of mankind may never rise beyond a *religious* appreciation of the truth about spirit as absolute reconciliation. They may experience a satisfaction in their simple religious faith which is adequate to the requirements of their common-sense level of consciousness. This religious fulfilment is a valid human experience and by no means to be despised. However, precisely because man is a thinking being he will not be fully liberated until through philosophical reflection he witnesses to spirit in the higher form of philosophy which discloses the rational necessity of the whole reconciling movement of the life of spirit. Only in this form is the fully adequate self-consciousness of spirit attained.[48]

At the close of our discussion of Kant's philosophy of God we anticipated that Hegel's philosophy, by reconciling in a higher synthesis a theocentric and anthropocentric view of the source of meaning and value, would attempt to overcome the suggestion that the affirmation of God is a source of human alienation. In the present chapter we have provided an outline of this endeavour. We have seen how Hegel passed from his early attempts to provide a romantic and essentially religious resolution of the apparently alienating features of Christianity to a specifically rational and philosophical treatment of the whole problem of the finite-infinite relationship. In this philosophy, which comprehends reality in its entirety as the auto-generation of infinite spirit which comes to fulfilment only through a process of self-estrangement and self-recovery in the various dimensions of finitude, we have seen how Hegel provides a speculative resolution of all oppositions and alienations. In particular man is deemed to be rescued, in principle, from the grip of alienation when all dimensions of his activity, including religious belief, are comprehended philosophically in their inner significance as moments of the life of absolute spirit. This philosophical comprehension discloses both the root of all alienation in the necessary self-estrangement of spirit and also its assured resolution in the development of spirit to adequate self-consciousness through philosophy itself.

The mainspring of this speculative conquest of alienation is a transformation of the conceptions of both God and man within the more comprehensive notion of absolute spirit. God is now conceived as comprising finitude as a necessary phase of His auto-constitution as spirit. Correlatively, man is no longer conceived as a contingent reality gratuitously 'divinised' by divine adoption but rather as 'divine' in his own right as a necessary feature of the development of the life of spirit. Theism, with its allegedly irreducibly alienating conceptions of man and God, has been transcended in the new encompassing philosophical context of spirit.

Hegel's remarkable system represents the apex of modern philosophical thought about God. In the majestic sweep of its interpretative virtuosity, in its assimilation and transformation of earlier thought and in its power of inspiration it is comparable on the *philosophical* level with the great *theological* synthesis which Aquinas achieved for medieval thought. Within an original conceptual framework it provides a unified theory of Being, of Thought and of God, which has enriched and deepened the subsequent course of reflection upon the divine nature. Even those who for one reason or another would not accept the Hegelian synthesis have been compelled, by its original and illuminating restatement of traditional doctrine, to reach beyond the formality of the long-accepted definitions to a keener appreciation of their inadequacy as expressions of the mystery which they signify. Hegel's philosophy has unquestionably been a challenge to theological complacency and a powerful stimulus to refinement and renewal of theological understanding. Paradoxically, however, as the following chapters will illustrate, it has also been one of the most influential sources of contemporary atheism. Contrary to its author's intention it paved the way for an explicit denial of God and a renewed and more radical affirmation of the view that belief in God is a source of human alienation.

It can be argued that the various forms of contemporary atheism such as Marxism, Positivism and Existentialism are not simply reactions against Hegel's philosophy of spirit but also and more profoundly progressive refinements of an atheism already laid down if not explicitly recognised in this philosophy. For example, a Christian commentator might take issue with Hegel's claim that philosophy presents in the superior *form* of rational necessity the same *content* as that expressed in religious affirmations. He could argue that the project of expressing the content of Christianity in the form of rational necessity inevitably involves a perversion of the content itself. For the content of Christian revelation describes a sacred history of the free and unnecessitated communication of God with man which resists Hegel's claim that 'the true Christian content of faith is to be justified by philosophy, not by history'.[49]

The religious representation of particular historical events as arising solely from the divine wisdom and sovereign freedom attributes to the events as such a significance which is irreducible to philosophical reformulation in terms of strict rational necessitation.[50] Hegel's attempt to effect such a reformulation will be seen as undermining the true religious representation of the Christian God by subordinating it to an ideal of philosophical explanation which is incompatible with the explicit content of this religious representation itself.

The content of the religious representation portrays man as basically receptive of the divine initiative of God's free and 'eventful' work of salvation. Hegel's philosophy claims to transcend this human perspective on the finite-infinite relationship and to comprehend the relationship from a divine viewpoint through an adequate speculative re-enactment of it. If, as Hegel maintains, this divine viewpoint is accessible to man and if the divine self-knowledge which it involves is realised only through man's philosophical consciousness, then the Christian religion is falsified in its content no less than in its form. For in Christian religious representation the finite order is understood as being, in its whole reality, divinely willed and personally 'intended' existence. It is not enough, from the religious standpoint, that the finite order be understood to be such that it can, in the person of man, intend an infinite trinitarian ideal of rationality. The finite order must itself be understood as *intended by* an actual divine Trinity. In other words, it would be claimed that the affirmation of God rests upon the assertion of the absolute ontological priority of an act of *actually intending rationality* rather than on a Hegelian ideal of rationality which is capable of being intended through the philosophical resolve which wills pure thought. Hence, the believer would argue that in Hegel's system the central content of religion has been either discredited or misrepresented in its philosophical reformulation and not, as Hegel would wish to maintain, merely purified.

In more general terms, it could be argued that Hegel's conception of philosophy, as total reflection which adequately comprehends the complete rational necessity of an all-embracing absolute spirit, can sustain its affirmation of God and religion only in virtue of a systematic ambiguity. For, as has been indicated above, the identifying properties of 'God' such as 'absolute transcendence', 'unlimited freedom' and 'immutable perfection', are used in such a radically transformed sense to describe the nature of absolute spirit that the continued use of the term 'God' in this context is more misleading than illuminating. Subsequent forms of explicit atheism can be said to have been mediated primarily through a refinement of the Hegelian conception of the absolute which divests it of inappropriate religious connotations and false pretensions to a divine significance. Thus, as we shall see, both Marxism and Positivism can each, in different ways, be considered as embodying a naturalised conception of the Hegelian absolute. This process of demythologising culminates in atheistic Existentialism with its repudiation of the idea of an absolute in any form.

It would, of course, be a serious oversimplification to explain the various forms of contemporary atheism as merely progressive resolutions of the inherent ambiguities of Hegelian philosophy. Other currents of thought and significant historical developments at every level of human endeavour have contributed their due share to shaping the different profiles of atheism. However, in retrospect one can see the decisive importance of Hegel's philosophy of spirit as providing a new total metaphysical viewpoint by reference to which the different forms of atheism could come to formulate and clarify their own significance.

Moreover, Hegel's analysis of human alienation and his explicit conviction that its most grievous source is a false conception of God have also exercised a profound influence upon the subsequent development of various forms of philosophical atheism. These themes have been reaffirmed not merely along the lines of Hegel's approach but also, and even more devastatingly, against his own conception of the true relationship between man and God. Thus it has been argued that the depths of human alienation which Hegel analysed so well can only be transmuted into authentic existence, not by affirming the ultimate unity of man and God as the absolute truth, but rather by rejecting God and affirming man as the only absolute.

This viewpoint is well illustrated in the thought of Feuerbach and Marx. Each in his own way was much impressed by Hegel's argument that a servile religious conception of man will inevitably be accompanied by an alienated social and political condition. But they insisted that instead of proposing, as Hegel had done, a basically ineffectual resolution of the problem in terms of a mystifying philosophical theory of the ultimate unity of man and God, it must be tackled rather in terms of a thoroughgoing explicit atheism. In the following two chapters we will consider this contention as it finds expression in the thought of Feuerbach and Marx respectively.

4

Feuerbach and the Apotheosis of Man

LUDWIG FEUERBACH (1804–1872) commenced his academic career as a student of Protestant theology at the University of Heidelberg. Subsequently he transferred to the University of Berlin where he became an enthusiastic disciple of Hegel whose lectures he regularly attended. Eventually, however, his personal reflections led him to discard both theology and Hegel's philosophy and to elaborate an explicitly atheistic philosophy of man involving a conscious transformation of the Hegelian viewpoint. As Karl Barth, whose own theological views developed in large measure as a reply to Feuerbach's philosophy, remarks: 'having proceeded far beyond Hegel as well as Kant, Feuerbach belongs to the Berlin master's disciples who scented the theological residue in his teaching and stripped it off.'[1] He seeks to provide an anti-theological interpretation of religion which will establish, as the truth behind the appearance, that fundamentally religion believes in and worships not God but human nature conceived as in itself the divine or supreme perfection. Thus his chief work, *The Essence of Christianity* (1841), which immediately established his reputation as the most celebrated and discussed German philosopher of the decade, is divided into two parts. The first is a positive one exhibiting the true essence of religion, the second a negative one discrediting the claims of all theology. He conceived his task as one of showing that 'the antithesis of divine and human is altogether illusory, that it is nothing else than the antithesis between the human nature in general and the human individual; that, consequently, the object and contents of the Christian religion are altogether human.'[2]

According to Feuerbach, the basis of religion must be sought in the essential difference between man and brute animals, for the latter have no religion. This difference is man's consciousness of himself not just as an individual but in his essential nature or as pertaining to a species. It is because his own *specific* nature can be an object of thought for man that he is in general capable of science, which is knowledge of species. Moreover, because his species or essential nature is an object of thought for man he can be said to transcend his individual limitations and thus attain to a consciousness of the infinite. The basis of religion in man's distinctive characteristic now becomes evident. In effect, religion, which is described generally as consciousness of the infinite, is to be understood as the consciousness which man has of his own infinite nature. Further, by implication, this consciousness of the infinite is 'nothing else than the consciousness of the infinity of consciousness'.[3] For it is in virtue of the unrestricted nature of his consciousness that man transcends the limitations and particularity of merely brute animal existence and can live in relation to his species, to his general, as distinguished from his individual, nature.

The proper constituent elements of the essential nature of man are the absolute self-authenticating attributes of reason, will and love. 'That alone is true, perfect, divine, which exists for its own sake. But such is love, such is reason, such is will. Reason, Will, Love are not powers which man possesses, for he is nothing without them, he is what he is only by them; they are the constituent elements of his nature, which he neither has nor makes, the animating, determining, governing powers—divine absolute powers—to which he can oppose no resistance.'[4] Whatever our individual shortcomings and limitations, we recognise reason, will and love as in themselves infinite unqualified perfections. They are characteristics which are ends in themselves. We think, will and love simply for the sake of reason, freedom of will, and love.

Each person as an individual human being recognises himself to be limited and recognises his dependence upon Nature. But in also recognising the infinity of the human species, as characterised by perfections which transcend man simply as an individual—namely, reason, will and love—he attains an object of absolute worth. 'The *absolute* to man is his own nature.'[5]

However, a proper understanding of this infinity of his species is not directly attained by man. In fact he is prone to ascribe his own individual limitations to the species as such and to project the infinite perfection of his essence into an external object. In this way he comes to the 'religious' affirmation of God as infinite knowledge, will and love. Religion, in its pejorative sense, is man's earliest and in-direct form of self-knowledge in which he contemplates his own nature as though extrinsic to himself and pertaining rather to a transcendent deity. Religion represents the naive childlike condition of humanity which must be transmuted by philosophy into an integral humanism.

Thus, for Feuerbach, the religious man is by definition the alienated man. The crowning perfections of his essential nature he mistakenly ascribes to God and, by contrast with this extrapolation, defines himself in terms of the merely individual, the incidental, the imperfect. Since the religious projection is essentially a transference of human properties to an illusory God, the richer the notion of God elaborated, the more man is impoverished and reduced to a miserable and servile condition. 'Religion is the disuniting of man from himself; he sets God before him as the antithesis of himself. God is not what man is—man is not what God is. God is the infinite, man the finite being; God is perfect, man imperfect; God eternal, man temporal; God almighty, man weak; God holy, man sinful. God and man are extremes: God is the absolutely positive, the sum of all realities; man the absolutely negative, comprehending all negations.'[6] This false antithesis must be resolved, not in the illusory way of Hegel's philosophy of spirit, but in a manner which will genuinely liberate man and reconcile him with his true reality.

The fundamental weakness of Hegel's philosophical approach is that he sought to eliminate human alienation and achieve a reconciliation of man and God through a theory which on reflection can be seen to be biased in favour of God at the expense of man. He thereby merely compounded the alienation under the appearance of resolving it. He advanced a theory which inverts the true relationship of subject and predicate by affirming a divine subject of certain perfections rather than predicating divinity of the perfections themselves. Thus he provides merely a speculative idealistic solution to a problem which, in fidelity to the human context, should be tackled concretely and empirically. He assimilates human consciousness to divine consciousness in such a way that man's consciousness of God is interpreted in terms of God's consciousness of Himself. This is simply a prolongation of and total capitulation to the religious illusion whereas what is required is its reversal and radical overthrow in a theory which interprets man's consciousness of God in terms of man's consciousness of himself. 'Why then dost thou alienate man's consciousness from him, and make it the self-consciousness of a being distinct from man, of that which is an object to him? . . . Man's knowledge of God is God's knowledge of himself? What a divorcing and contradiction! The true statement is this: man's knowledge of God is man's knowledge of himself, of his own nature.'[7]

According to Feuerbach the key to the ultimate truth about man is a rigorous application of the principle that the real object and adequate basis of any meaning and value disclosed to human consciousness is human nature itself. It is because the nature of human consciousness is such as it is that objects appear to us, and affect us, as they do. An object of any form of human consciousness, e.g. feeling, sensibility, understanding, will, is always in its inner significance an objectification of human nature. 'Thus the power of the object of feeling is the power of feeling itself; the power of the object of the intellect is the power of the intellect itself; the power of the object of the will is the power of the will itself.'[8] We live in an irreducibly human milieu. Any concrete attempt to envisage an absolute order of meaning and value transcending our human context and resources is in its very exercise a fantasy and a self-defeating project.

Feuerbach's principle that the significance of an object of consciousness is to be understood in terms of its psycho-genesis from human nature itself is extensively applied to achieve his aim of explaining the essence of religion and reducing all theology to anthropology. This programme of secularisation signalises the triumph of an uncompromising humanism of liberty which has haunted philosophical reflection like an unfulfilled promise ever since Descartes' fateful explorations into human subjectivity for the roots of meaning and value. To illustrate the form in which it eventually came to realisation in the philosophy of Feuerbach let us consider briefly some salient features of his critical analysis of religion and its correlative conception of man.

According to Feuerbach the object of religious consciousness is of central importance for disclosing the ultimate significance of human nature. For in religion consciousness intends the divine, that which is to be worshipped as the supreme perfection, and thus discloses, admittedly in an alienated form of awareness, the innermost core of the human reality. In the notion of God as object of religious consciousness we find a fantasy expression of man's ideal of human excellence. Through a progressive refinement and spiritual enrichment of the notion of God, the historical evolution of religion has worked towards the eventual disclosure of a truly fundamental conception of man. The evolution from the mere personification of natural forces in nature religions to a deity characterised by spiritual and ethical properties reflects the movement of human development from a state of savagery and wildness to one of culture. However, even the most developed form of religion remains subject to the inevitable illusion of religious consciousness in general, namely, that it supposes its object to be a super-human reality. Only when religion as such is itself made an object of philosophical reflection can a true understanding of its essence be achieved.

A vital step in attaining this understanding is a realisation that in religion what is really revered is not the alleged subject of divine attributes but rather the divinity of the attributes themselves. It is what a man judges to be the supreme perfection that he holds to be divine. Thus, for example, if the pagan gods were conceived in terms of sensual appetites, physical prowess, or heroic qualities, it was because these were the attributes which were held in the highest esteem as worthy of veneration. The viewpoint which pretends to exalt God's existence by asserting the inadequacy of any of our inevitably human predicates to represent Him as He is in Himself is equivalent to a subtle form of atheism. For all practical purposes a being devoid of qualities is effectively non-existent—a mere empty thought. 'The denial of determinate, positive predicates concerning the divine nature is nothing else than a denial of religion, with, however, an appearance of religion in its favour, so that it is not recognised as a denial; it is simply a subtle, disguised atheism.'[9]

Moreover, the distinction between God as He is in Himself and God as He is for me is untenable. I can assert nothing whatsoever about God other than as He is for me. So far as I am concerned, what God is for me is all that God is in Himself. The distinction between an object as it is in itself and as it is for me has some point only when the object can really appear otherwise to me than it does. It is illusory transcendentalism to speak of a distinction between an object such as it must appear to me and such as it is in itself in a way which I could never know.

Further, what God is for me is totally conveyed in the predicates through which I conceive Him as supreme perfection. There is no valid basis for the supposition that the affirmation of the existence of a divine subject is somehow more certain and less anthropomorphic than the predicates which describe Him. If one doubts the objective validity of the predicates attributed to a divine subject one must also doubt the objectivity of the subject of these predicates. If the predicates in question such as love, goodness, personality, etc., are anthropomorphisms, merely human ways of envisaging the divine, so also is the affirmation of the existence of their divine subject merely an anthropomorphic way of envisaging reality. Thus, for example, how could one be sure that the affirmation of the existence of God is not simply a limitation or perversion of the human mode of conception which would be eliminated in a more enlightened form of consciousness?[10]

Hence, in our consideration of religion and its divine object we should be guided by the principle that 'what the subject is lies only in the predicate; the predicate is the *truth* of the subject—the subject only the personified, existing predicate, the predicate conceived as existing.'[11] This principle enables us to achieve a proper understanding of religion and a clearer insight into the fact that the divine attributes have their basis exclusively in human nature. The God of religion will then be seen to be an extrapolation of the essential attributes of human nature regarded as absolute truth. We will, moreover, rid ourselves effectively of all the deceptions and mystifications of theology. For, whereas religion embodies merely a pre-reflective projection of human attributes onto an illusory divine being, theology compounds this alienation by taking the transcendent divine subject onto whom the human attributes have been projected as the absolute and veridical starting point of its reflections.[12] Such theological illusion and its consequences will be avoided when we

F

appreciate that the divine subject is reducible to its defining attributes and that these are projections of specifically human qualities.

The mystery of religion is that man projects his innermost subjectivity into objectivity and converts the resulting image into a transcendent subject or God. In the more developed forms of religion, and notably in Christianity, this God is portrayed in richly personal and ethical categories. The detached metaphysical conception of the divine being as supreme intelligence provides merely the speculative under-pinning for the essentially affective attributes of the God of religion such as moral Lawgiver and loving Father. It is to the affective exigencies of concrete human subjectivity for moral rectitude and salvific reconciliation, rather than to the demands of disinterested rational reflection, that God as an object of religious consciousness properly corresponds. Hence, notwithstanding the efforts of speculative theology to obscure the issue, the God of religion is necessarily anthropomorphic. For only as strictly correlative to these existential dimensions of human subjectivity is God genuinely relevant to religious consciousness. Only a specifically human God, a God not wholly other than man but rather sharing with him a common nature and common properties, could be of interest to specifically human concerns. 'In religion man seeks contentment; religion is his highest good. But how could he find consolation and peace in God if God were an essentially different being? . . . If his nature is different from mine, his peace is essentially different,—it is no peace for me.'[13]

According to Feuerbach, Christianity, as distinct from misleading theological versions of it, portrays God through specifically human predicates. Moreover, it can be trans-formed into a true philosophy of man once it has been purified of a) the religious illusion of ascribing divinity primarily to a supposed subject rather than to the predicated perfections, and b) the closely related error of affirming the infinity of the species only in the alienated form of a divine infinite individual because of a false identification of species and individual.

Thus, for example, the Christian mystery of the Incarnation speaks to man of God as unselfish love for man. Its basic elements are God and love. What is truly worshipful in this mystery is not a divine subject who loves but rather the absolute 'divine' perfection of unselfish love itself. 'What then is the true unfalsified import of the Incarnation but absolute, pure love, without adjunct, without a distinction between divine and human love? For though there is also a self-interested love among men, still the true human love, which is alone worthy of this name, is that which impels sacrifice of self to another. Who then is our Saviour and Redeemer? God or Love? Love; for God as God has not saved us, but Love, which transcends the difference between the divine and human personality.'[14]

Feuerbach provides a similar reductive transformation of other features of Christian belief. For example, he describes the mystery of the Trinity as revealing in an alienated religious way the absolute or divine character of self-consciousness. It is also seen as illustrating the truth that adequate self-consciousness is mediated only through the I-Thou relationship of community life. 'Participated life is alone true, self-satisfying, divine life:—this simple thought, this truth, natural, immanent in man, is the secret, the supernatural mystery of the Trinity.'[15]

Likewise he argues that the divine power of language as a fundamental principle of human perfection and liberation is intimated in the theme of the Word of God. The worship of the Word of God is an indirect acknowledgement of the divine power of human language as it becomes an object to man in the sphere of religion.[16] In a similar manner he claims that the doctrine of the creation of the world through the second Person depicts in a religious way the truth that man enters into a meaningful 'world-building' relationship with his natural environment only through the cultural mediation of his fellow-man. It depicts the supreme significance of inter-subjectivity as a source of human perfection. 'The *ego* then, attains to consciousness of the world through consciousness of the *thou*. Thus man is the God of man. . . . In isolation human power is limited, in combination it is infinite.'[17]

It is unnecessary to dwell upon the details of Feuerbach's analysis of these and other features of Christian belief. The central theme which pervades the entire analysis is sufficiently clear, namely, that religion is essentially an alienated form of self-awareness, an illusion which must be overcome by tracing it back to its true source and object—the absolute nature of man. God is merely the objectification of human subjectivity released from incidental individual limitations. Religion acknowledges the species properties of man, his essential humanity, but mistakenly converts them into a divine being distinct from man. The inner truth of faith in God is man's faith in the infinitude and absolute freedom of his own nature. The anthropological reduction of religion brings this truth to the forefront of human consciousness and rescues man from his religious self-alienation. Thus in a concluding appraisal of his achievement Feuerbach observes: 'We have reduced the supermundane, supernatural, and superhuman nature of God to the elements of human nature as its fundamental elements. Our process of analysis has brought us again to the position with which we set out. The beginning, middle and end of religion is MAN.'[18]

Let us now consider in broad outline the conception of man which emerges from this transformation of religion and theology into anthropology. According to Feuerbach, having dispelled belief in God as the divine subject of infinite self-authenticating perfections, we are able to bring these perfections 'down to earth' into their basic human setting. The true human reality is the species, the human race, collective man—not idealised and projected as a divine individual—but in its concrete life as a historically evolving ensemble, of which each individual man, as individual, is but a transitory moment.

The true reconciliation of finite and infinite is not an abstract reconciliation of man with the merely thought perfection of an absolute divine subject. It is rather a social, lived reconciliation of individual limited man with the absolute perfection of the human species. The individual attains an absolute and guaranteed significance through participation in the collective perfection of the species whose unlimited virtuality transcends the resources of the mere individual.

All divine attributes, all the attributes which make God God, are attributes of the species—attributes which in the individual are limited, but the limits of which are abolished in the essence of the species, and even in its existence, in so far as it has its complete existence only in all men taken together. My knowledge, my will, is limited; but my limit is not the limit of another man, to say nothing of mankind; what is difficult to me is easy to another; what is impossible, inconceivable, to one age, is to the coming age conceivable and possible. My life is bound to a limited time; not so the life of humanity.[19]

Thus, in conscious opposition to the idealist tradition, Feuerbach proposes what he calls a 'materialist' or 'realist' resolution of the problem of human alienation. He tells us that he is an idealist only in the ethical and practical sense that he firmly believes we participate in the assured eventual reality of the triumph and reign of absolute values such as truth, freedom, justice and love. But as regards the form in which, and the means whereby, the absolute reconciliation of man with his true reality is to be accomplished he is unequivocally and exclusively committed to a 'this worldly' naturalistic humanism. The reconciliation takes the form of each man's participation in the progressive constitution of the infinite perfection of humanity as a concrete and complex totality. This goal is achieved through the communal historical development of material, biological, ethical and cultural relationships.

Feuerbach's account of man as a species being is advanced as a corrective to philosophical individualism generally and to the individualism of religion in particular. For he claims that in religion, particularly the Christian religion, each man supposes himself to attain his essential perfection by himself alone through his personal contemplative relationship with a divine individual who is invested with all the universal perfection of the species. Because of this identification of the perfection of the human species with a divine individual, historical humanity is sacrificed to a transcendental illusion and the individual is estranged from his only effective context of fulfilment. Feuerbach's doctrine that essentially each man is not an individual but a species being—a being who enters into his humanity only in virtue of his mutually sustaining relationships with other men—is intended to point the way towards a practical accomplishment of human fulfilment, as distinct from the illusory salvation of religious individualism.[20]

According to Feuerbach this absolute reality of man as inter-subjectivity, as coming to his truth in the community of the species, is mediated primarily, not through the abstract domain of thought, but through the lived biological domain of sexuality. The estrangement and limitation of the individual as such *vis-à-vis* the species is most clearly experienced through the awareness of sexual differentiation. Man and woman are reciprocally dependent upon their mutual complementarity for the achievement of their specific reality. Only man and woman together first constitute the true man. Taken together they are the prototype of humanity. For their union is the source of multiplicity, the source of other men, the primary embodiment of humanity.

From within this difference of sex evolves the self-sufficient infinite perfection of love which transcends the limitations of individuals and branches out in different dimensions to bring about the self-consciousness of the species as a complex community of hierarchically ordered interpersonal relationships.[21] Through this structured articulation of love we come to a developed awareness that our humanity is grounded in our lived historical relationships with our fellow men. 'In another I first have the consciousness of humanity; through him I first learn, I first feel, that I am a man: in my love for him it is first clear to me that he belongs to me and I to him, that we two cannot be without each other, that only community constitutes humanity.'[22] Hence, the reconciliation of man with the absolute, i.e. with the sacred reality of his species, is achieved not through interior communion with a religious projection of the species in the form of a divine infinite individual but through the loving solidarity of men in their secular life. Thus 'there *is* a natural reconciliation. My fellow-man is *per se* the mediator between me and the sacred reality of the species. *Homo homini Deus est.*'[23]

If one refuses to characterise as atheism any view which affirms the reality of an absolute in any form whatsoever, and if one is prepared to count as religion reverential commitment to an absolute howsoever conceived, then there are grounds for asserting that Feuerbach's philosophy involves neither atheism nor a rejection of religion. For he affirms the infinite perfection of the human species as an absolute worthy of unqualified reverence. Further, there are various texts which suggest that he is willing to be understood as retaining the affirmation of God and religion in this special sense. For example, he observes that even eating and drinking are to be conceived as religious activities which should put us gratefully in mind of man the divine reality who satisfies our needs.[24]

However, this somewhat elastic conception of divine reality and religion tends to obscure rather than clarify the discussion of the problem of God. Moreover, to lend any special significance to this feature of Feuerbach's thought might deflect attention from his main thesis, namely, an explicit and total rejection of God and religion as usually understood, and an unqualified denial of any trans-human absolute principle of meaning and value such as Hegel's absolute spirit.

Perhaps the most significant feature of Feuerbach's philosophy is that, after the various attempts of Descartes, Kant and Hegel to combine the immanentism of the epistemological tradition deriving from the *cogito* with an affirmation of supra-natural Being, it clearly maintains that the natural world of empirical reality is the limiting horizon of human consciousness and existence. Thus the atheism potential in this tradition is brought explicitly to light.[25]

In his own way Feuerbach is faithful to the perspective of the *cogito* tradition according to which the world is constituted as a world of meaning and value only through the activity of human consciousness. He maintains that the object of consciousness is always an objectification of man's subjective nature. However, he combines this view with explicit doctrines of materialism and realism which accord an irreducible primacy to sense experience and confine the resources of human nature, including its field of consciousness, to the context of spatio-temporal existence. The result, as we have seen, is a thoroughgoing naturalistic humanism in which the absolute is identified with human nature which in turn is interpreted in exclusively socio-historical terms.

Feuerbach's thought is scarcely a model of rigorous and conclusive philosophical analysis. In general its mode of expression is literary rather than strictly philosophical, relying often on the illuminating aphorism instead of detailed critical argument. For example, the compatibility of his sense materialism with his view of the field of consciousness as an objectification of human subjectivity is not convincingly worked out. As one commentator observes: 'Feuerbach does believe with Protagoras that *man is the measure of all things—* though he also believes that things exist independently of man and that we cannot consider one without the other. Here, of course, is a source of much unexamined difficulty, reflected in the imprecision of Feuerbach's discussion of the relation between "man" and "nature", just as it was reflected in the imprecision of his discussion of the relation between thought and body, and of the relation between understanding and sense-experience.'[26]

Likewise there is a certain ambiguity in his reduction of the qualitative 'infinity' of such absolute perfections as truth, freedom, justice and love, to the quantitative 'infinity' of their varied empirical realisations throughout the collective history of the species.[27] If these perfections are thus reducible merely to their combined *de facto* exemplifications throughout human history it is not evident how Feuerbach can justify his further and related contention that these perfections are intrinsically such that they must eventually transcend the vicissitudes of their present limited condition and come to prevail in a perfect form as the assured fulfilment of human striving for a reign of truth and virtue.

In a somewhat analogous manner his theory of the psychogenesis of the idea of God is not really adequate to its aim of disposing of theism. In seeking to resolve a metaphysical problem in psychological terms it strikes one as merely presenting a polemical account of how we might have come by the idea of a God who is *assumed* not to exist, rather than as disclosing objective grounds for the denial of his existence. The whole nature and existence of religious worship of God is thought to be adequately understood in terms of a theory of the necessary psychological conditions of its possibility. The falsity of belief in God is supposedly established by an account of how we might have come to have such a belief.

Nevertheless, notwithstanding its shortcomings, Feuerbach's philosophy undoubtedly constitutes an important chapter in the formation of contemporary atheism. It marks the definite arrival of a fully consciously formulated atheism. It does not simply propose a theory of the ultimate meaning of reality which on reflection is seen to be atheistic. Rather it deliberately advocates an explicit atheism as a necessary prolegomenon to a true appraisal of reality in general and human existence in particular. It eliminates any reference to God as always and intrinsically a source of alienation and mystification which must be dispelled if human integrity is to be achieved.

Furthermore, by eliminating the context of the supra-natural, this philosophy is enabled to direct the quest for ultimate meaning and value exclusively within the limits of the natural, the human and the social. Thus these categories take on a heightened importance and interest as constituting the only relevant domain in which man can seek for a principle of absolute significance and authenticity. As new insights and possibilities are disclosed by concentration of attention within this new confined area of interest, the problem of God will become one of increasingly marginal concern. Atheism will appear more and more as in no way remarkable but rather the natural presupposition of civilised man.

In effect, the philosophy of Feuerbach can be regarded as one which attuned human consciousness to a strictly and explicitly atheistic world-view, even though it may also be considered as only laying down the main lines of such a viewpoint in a somewhat rudimentary form. The interest of subsequent philosophers, as we shall illustrate in our discussion of Marxism, Positivism and Existentialism, would be absorbed in seeking to provide ever more penetrating and sophisticated versions of this newly established and readily accepted outlook.

5

Marx and Secular Salvation

T H E explicitly atheistic humanism of Feuerbach was deepened and energised in the philosophy of Karl Marx (1818–1883), which proposed a revolutionary and dynamic conception of man, society and history. The subsequent course of events, in virtue of which Marxism has become a powerful ideology of global dimensions, has made this philosophy one of the most influential sources of contemporary atheism. This chapter will treat of the thought of Marx himself in so far as it bears upon the theme of atheism and alienation. We will be concerned chiefly with the early period of his thought up to the publication of *The Manifesto of the Communist Party* in 1848. For by comparison with the specifically scientific and impersonal orientation of his later writings the early Marx is more interested in the philosophical issues of human destiny and authenticity and the correct appraisal of religious belief.

From the very outset of his career, when he was associated with the Young Hegelians who applied Hegel's philosophy in the direction of a radical critique of religion and politics, Marx was a convinced atheist. In his earliest writings atheism is affirmed as an essential feature of his conception of man. Thus in his doctoral thesis of 1841 he emphatically asserts that the supreme reality is man not God.[1]

Two aspects of the atheism of Marx should be distinguished. On the one hand, there is his direct critique of religion interpreted as a form of alienation. On the other hand, there is a positive theory of man incorporating a programme of action which, it is claimed, will effectively eliminate the problem of God by overcoming at their source all manifestations of human alienation. It envisages a state of affairs in which there will be quite simply a non-problematical absence of God in the minds and hearts of men. There is, as we shall see, an intimate connection between these two aspects of Marxist atheism. The critical aspect renders possible the positive theory of man and this, in turn, unfolds itself as the vindication and ultimate verification of the critique of religion. Let us consider each of these two aspects.

Perhaps the first point which should be noted in reference to Marx's critique of religion is that it is not metaphysically orientated. Thus, for example, his writings reveal no great interest in a purely theoretical analysis and critique of traditional proofs for the existence of God. On the rare occasions on which he does direct his thought to such topics his treatment is brief and not particularly profound. For instance, he argues that to raise the question of a creator of the world and of man is to pose a pseudo-question. For, in virtue of a pointless abstraction, it supposes the world and man as previously non-existent and demands a demonstration of their existence. But such an abstraction negates the questioner himself and with him his question. In other words, 'if you want to maintain your abstraction, be consistent, and if you think of man and nature as non-existent, think of yourself too as non-existent, for you are also man and nature. Do not think, do not ask me any questions, for as soon as you think and ask questions your abstraction from the existence of nature and man becomes meaningless. Or are you such an egoist that you conceive everything as non-existent and yet want to exist yourself?'[2]

This contention that in talk about creation one is absurdly trying to ask questions from within a hypothetical context of non-being which eliminates the reality of any questioner is scarcely an impressive refutation of the traditional conception of creation. For traditionally the notion of creation was advanced primarily, not in order to derive a historical origin of man and nature from a supposed anterior state of non-being, but rather to explain the limitation and contingency of their existence here and now.

However, Marx was not interested in pursuing strictly metaphysical refinements. Nor would he have accepted that his indifference to the metaphysical mode of thought is an indication of the superficiality of his own critical method. On the contrary, he would argue that eventually his critique not only effectively undermines religion but also disposes of the illusory pretensions of all detached metaphysical reflection.

The notion of 'critique' is of central importance in Marx's thought. Its role is the progressive disclosure of the nature and ultimate source of the manifold alienations of man. Animated by an ideal of human liberation, which envisages the harmonious integration of man and nature and the effective recognition of man by man, Marx's critique is directed against the various dimensions of ideology through which existing society understands itself and explains itself to itself. It consists in showing that at the various levels of ideological self-explanation—religious, philosophical, political, social and economic—society deceives itself and conceals the truth about man. It presents man to himself in terms which distort the true ideal of human liberation and conceal the misery of his actual condition. Thus in its various forms it constitutes an estrangement or alienation of man from himself.

Marx's programme of critique is proposed in order to uncover the depth of human alienation embodied in the mystifications of ideology and thereby to clarify man's true goal and the means to its accomplishment. According to him a critique of religion is the proper starting point in this general critique of ideology. In his own words: 'the criticism of religion is the premise of all criticism.'[3]

For Marx the critique of religion enjoys a privileged position in a general critique of ideological mystification, not because it is its most fundamental source, but because it is its crowning and most palliative manifestation. Unmask religion as a form of alienation and man will more readily advert to other, and ultimately more pernicious, dimensions of his estrangement. 'The criticism of religion is, therefore, *the embryonic criticism of this vale of tears* of which religion is the *halo*.'[4]

According to Marx the basis of a critique of religion is a recognition of the fact that '*man makes religion;* religion does not make man'.[5] In developing this basic theme he endorses the view of Feuerbach that religion is essentially a form of human consciousness which reflects an estranged human condition. It is the heavenly counterpart of an inauthentic secular existence. More specifically, it is at once an expression of and a protest against an inhuman state of society. 'This state, this society, produce religion which is an *inverted world consciousness,* because they are an inverted world. . . . It is *the fantastic realisation* of the human being inasmuch as the *human being* possesses no true reality.'[6] However, as a form of protest it is ineffectual. For it merely provides a deceptive justification and illusory consolation for an unhappy state of human society.

Marx interprets various historical manifestations of religious practice as empirical confirmation of his contention that religion inculcates unavailing other-worldly resignation to the *status quo.* Thus he speaks of the social principles of Christianity justifying the slavery of Antiquity, glorifying the serfdom of the Middle Ages, and defending the oppression of the proletariat. Further, he describes these principles as judging acts of oppression to be the just punishment for sin or trials imposed by God in His wisdom with a view to our redemption.[7]

If Marx's critique of religion were confined to the features which we have so far described it might be argued that his position is not intrinsically atheistic. Thus one might maintain that he was rejecting only the perversion of religion which can and does arise from a defective social order. It might be said that in appealing to particular historical instances to support his condemnation of religion as mystification he was not expanding empirical observations into a philosophical generalisation condemning *all* religion but simply illustrating the principle that inauthenticity in the secular order is inevitably reflected in religious consciousness. This position would leave open the possibility that the accomplishment of an authentic social order might be accompanied by authentic religion.

However, such an interpretation of Marx's position cannot be defended in the light of a more developed consideration of his critique of religion and other aspects of his thought. For he criticises religion not only inasmuch as it is a reflection of and a futile protest against a given state of secular alienation but also as always in itself constituting a further specific dimension of alienation in virtue of which man is more than ever separated from himself.

The thesis which animates this conviction of Marx that religion is intrinsically alienating is one which we have seen being gradually articulated since the origins of modern thought and becoming unequivocally explicit in the philosophy of Feuerbach. It is the thesis that any attempt to explain man in terms of a principle allegedly superior to man himself constitutes an alienation of human autonomy. 'A being does not regard himself as independent unless he is his own master, and he is only his own master when he owes his existence to himself. A man who lives by the favour of another considers himself a dependent being. But I live completely by another person's favour when I owe to him not only the continuance of my life but also *its creation*; when he is its *source*'.[8] Hence, Marx accepts without reservation that the critique of religion must be total and radical—to the point of affirming man as the only absolute. 'Religion is only the illusory sun about which man revolves so long as he does not revolve about himself.'[9] Effective human emancipation is possible only if 'one adopts the point of view of that theory according to which man is the highest being for man'.[10]

Marx recognised that an effective verification of his critique of religion required an elaboration and justification of its humanist basis. The contention involved in this critique, namely that an affirmation of God as a being distinct from and superior to man is intrinsically alienating, rests on the assumption that reality admits of and requires an exclusively immanent accomplishment of human autonomy and fulfilment. Unless this assumption or ideal can literally be made good the charge of alienation against religion would not be definitively proved.

Hence Feuerbach's account of how religion must be dissolved and explained in terms of its secular basis, is both superficial and ineffectual. For it is not enough merely to illustrate how religion can be considered as an illusory projection of a secular reality. To ground such a view it is necessary to provide a more searching analysis of the inherent tensions and contradictions of this secular basis itself which will explain why the religious projection can and does occur. Moreover it is unavailing to suppose that the religious illusion will automatically disappear as a consequence of a philosophical insight which proclaims that a merely natural bond of brotherly love is the basic principle of human integrity and unification. What is required is a more practical appraisal of how the secular order might be transformed by work and revolutionary activity so as to effectively eliminate the inhuman basis which at present gives rise to the religious illusion.

Thus, although he gives due credit to Feuerbach for his limited achievement in referring religion back to its secular source, Marx insists that: 'He overlooks the fact that after this work is completed the chief thing still remains to be done. For the fact that the secular foundation detaches itself from itself and establishes itself in the clouds as an independent realm is really only to be explained by the self-cleavage and self-contradictoriness of this secular basis. The latter must itself, therefore, first be understood in its contradiction, and then revolutionised in practice by the removal of the contradiction.'[11]

What, for Marx, constitutes this self-contradictoriness of the secular world which must be understood in its contradiction and then revolutionised in practice? In its simplest and most basic terms the contradiction is that man, who as a worker and a social being should find fulfilment in his work and in his social relationships, is in fact dehumanised through his work and deformed by his social relationships.

Marx argued that the modern liberal capitalist State, which posed as the protector of the common interest of all its citizens—the guardian of truth, liberty and justice—was not in fact what it claimed to be, but rather an instrument used by a particular section of society, the ruling class, to perpetuate its economic power. Likewise, he took the appalling conditions of the working class in the nineteenth century as a clear indication that the real significance of work had been abused and distorted. Work, which should function as a truly human source of self-realisation and social cohesion, had in fact been debased to the inhuman level of merchandise. In order to survive, the worker must sell his work to the capitalist who owns the means of production. Thus, through the expropriation of the fruits of his work the worker is estranged from himself and from his fellow-man over against whom he stands in a relation of class conflict and struggle. 'If he is related to the product of his labour, his objectified labour, as to an *alien*, hostile, powerful and independent object, he is related in such a way that another alien, hostile, powerful and independent man is the lord of this object. If he is related to his own activity as unfree activity, then he is related to it as activity in the service, and under the domination, coercion and yoke, of another man.'[12]

Thus we arrive at what, for Marx, is the radical and original source of man's unhappiness and alienation. It is the exploitation of man by man. In particular it is the expropriation by the owners of the means of production of the

G

surplus value produced by the workers. The various systema-
tised modalities of cultural life such as law, politics, philosophy and religion are merely ideological mystifications
which accompany this basic exploitation. 'Religion, the
family, the state, law, morality, science, art, etc. are only
particular forms of production and come under its general
law.'[13] They come into being as so many deceptive attempts
to rationalise, justify and alleviate the basic economic
estrangement of man. The mysterious feature of the history
of man is that he has been enslaved by an ideological illusion
of his own making.

However, behind this framework of ideological illusion
there is the increasingly intensified emergence of a historical
reality which belies the illusions of ideology and which
contains within itself the seeds of the conquest of ideology and
an end of alienation. This historical reality is the proletariat,
that ever increasing class of workers whose progressive
dehumanisation by the inexorable logic of capitalism clearly
reveals the corruption and inauthenticity of its whole
ideology. In the final analysis the true significance of
alienation and the real principle of its effective elimination
are disclosed, not by a process of detached thought, but by
the historical formation of a vast pool of humanity utterly
devoid of any human dignity or quality. Marx describes what
this situation demands in a remarkable passage. He writes

A class must be formed which has *radical chains*, a class
in civil society which is not a class of civil society, a class
which is the dissolution of all classes, a sphere of society
which has a universal character because its sufferings are
universal, . . . a sphere, finally which cannot emancipate
itself without emancipating itself from all the other spheres
of society, without, therefore, emancipating all these other
spheres, which is, in short, a *total loss* of humanity and which
can only redeem itself by a *total redemption of humanity*. This
dissolution of society, as a particular class, is the *proletariat*.[14]

In the light of this analysis of alienation Marx spells out an account of authentic human fulfilment which should inspire and guide the revolutionary activity of the proletariat in overcoming the contradiction of their secular existence. The new vision of man, of authentic man, involved in this account, embodies the really radical aspect of Marx's atheism. It is *a*-theistic in the literal sense that any reference to God or to religion is totally irrelevant to this vision of man. It is a dynamic conception of man which when fully lived out will prove so genuinely efficacious in reconciling man with himself that it will, according to Marx, constitute conclusive empirical confirmation of his critique of religion as self-alienation. It is a conception of man whose concrete verification will be the historical realisation of a communist society. In the language and life of such a society any reference to God will be obsolete, irrelevant, non-existent.

The fundamental and animating theme of this new conception of man is that everything about man, society and history is to be understood from the perspective of productive work in society. In other words man is to be considered exclusively as one who makes himself what he is through his productive work. Moreover, as productive work is necessarily a social activity, it is only in and through community or society that man can truly make himself.

Man emerges from nature and from a scarcely more than animal form of existence precisely in so far as through his productive work he transforms nature to satisfy his various needs. He makes himself human by cultivating and humanising the world through his labour. Through the work whereby he satisfies his basic physical and biological needs he prepares the ground for the emergence of more specifically social and cultural needs, which in turn are satisfied through work. He progressively fashions himself through a dialectical dialogue with nature—a dialogue made effective through the process of work. The limits of the possibilities of human work are the limits of the possibilities of man's world, man's history, man's society and man's destiny. The range and quality of his consciousness are determined by the extent and character of the practical control over nature which he has achieved through his work. The transition from a state of almost total domination by the forces of nature and a merely herd-like existence to an effective humanisation of nature and an authentic community existence is achieved through productive work.[15]

According to Marx man will remain alienated and estranged until he steadfastly adheres to this essential truth that any meaning or value which he has, or can have, comes about exclusively through his own work. This is why the critique of religion is so necessary. It enables man to get behind the illusory representations of his condition and come to an effective appreciation of his true origin and goal. 'The criticism of religion disillusions man so that he will think, act and fashion his reality as a man who has lost his illusions and regained his reason; so that he will revolve about himself as his own true sun.'[16]

Thus, for Marx, the fundamental perspective from which we must develop an understanding of the human condition is rigorously opposed to any religious interpretation of this condition. Man is the work of man—and it is precisely and exclusively through his own work that man creates man and accomplishes through his own resources complete liberation and fulfilment. Human work is the absolute source of all man's value, of the quality of his society and of the meaning of his history. In Marx's own words: 'the *whole of what is called world history* is nothing but the creation of man by human labour.'[17]

Marxism in its basic inspiration is an absolute humanism, a dynamic materialism. Any suggestion that man's work of self-realisation should be integrated into a wider and more fundamental context and be seen, for example, as a phase in the life of a Hegelian absolute spirit or as a finite participation in the infinite being of a transcendent creator, must be repudiated as illusory substitution of shadow for substance. For all such metaphysical and theological conceptions are merely derivative and provisional accompaniments of the process of man's self-creation through his work.

That means that we proceed not from what men say, fancy or imagine, nor from men as they are spoken of, thought, fancied, imagined in order to arrive from them at men of flesh and blood; we proceed from the really active men and see the development of the ideological reflexes and echoes of their real life-process as proceeding from that life-process. Even the nebulous images in the brain of men are necessary sublimates of their material, empirically observable, materially preconditioned, life-process. Thus, morals, religion, metaphysics and other forms of ideology, and the forms of consciousness corresponding to them no longer retain their apparent independence. They have no history, they have no development, but men, developing their material production and their material intercourse, with this, their reality, their thinking and the products of their thinking also change. It is not consciousness that determines life, but life that determines consciousness.[18]

The naturalistic humanism inherent in Marx's insistence that productive work is the absolute source of meaning and value receives further confirmation and specification in his account of the social character and role of such work. In effect, the true goal of work is the construction of a communist society. Productive work, which is inherently social, is authentically human precisely in the measure that it is executed as a social project, i.e. in so far as it is a community enterprise of humanising nature with a view to the effective humanisation of the community of workers. It is in and through communal endeavour that ever more effective means of production can be developed. These in turn enable us to achieve eventually the realisation and fulfilment of man as a community reality.

The universal quality of man will be truly achieved when everyone experiences the world as that which, through the combined work of man, has become the dwelling place of a community which embodies the adequate fulfilment of everyone's needs and allows the proper expression of everyone's capacities. Hitherto this happy state has not been possible and the course of past history would be more aptly described as the pre-history of humanity. For hitherto we have been dominated by the reign of economic necessity or scarcity, which engenders the system of private property in which the root source of all alienation finds expression.[19]

Moreover, modern industrial capitalist society, notwithstanding its almost unlimited capacity for production, impedes the realisation of the authentic communist society. This is because the means of production are held by the few who confiscate for their own benefit the fruits of the work of the vast majority. However, as the workers under the pressure of progressive alienation and dehumanisation become aware of their predicament, they will revolt, seize the means of production and, after a period of socialist adjustment under the dictatorship of the proletariat, bring to fruition a communist society.

In this communist society, which will be the embodiment of man's creation of himself, all men will find their complete and specifically human fulfilment. Released from the divisive realm of necessity and scarcity, and its attendant dimensions of alienation, every individual will enjoy the authentic liberation of entering into and cultivating his true reality as a species being. In his work he will experience himself as one impelled rather than as one compelled. The concept of 'need' will assume a positive significance so that 'the wealthy man is at the same time one who *needs* a complex of human manifestations of life, and whose self-realisation exists as an inner necessity, a *need*.'[20]

Work will no longer be experienced as a dehumanising competitive task in the service of individual survival but as the free and proper expression of man's accomplishment of himself as totally socialised. In his work man will enjoy a lived and fully satisfying appreciation of the exclusively 'this-worldly' and social significance of his life. Thus in such a society it will be acknowledged that 'activity in direct association with others has become an organ for the manifestation of life and a mode of appropriation of *human* life.'[21] At this developed level of human existence even the prospect of one's individual death will simply confirm one's conviction that one's true reality, even as an individual, is encompassed within the social milieu of one's species life and species consciousness.[22]

The state of affairs envisaged by Marx as the outcome of human praxis is a community of totally socialised and naturalised citizens of a truly humanised natural world. 'The *natural* existence of man has become his *human* existence and nature itself has become human for him. Thus *society* is the accomplished union of man with nature, the veritable resurrection of nature, the realised naturalism of man and the realised humanism of nature.'[23]

This communist society is not postulated as something over against the individual but rather as constituting the adequate fulfilment of the individual. However, although Marx thus acknowledges the significance of the individual as 'the subjective existence of society as thought and experienced',[24] it must be emphasised that, for him, this significance is exclusively social. It is solely in terms of the society by which he is borne and of which he is the bearer that the individual is significant. Hence, there is little if any scope in this conception for attributing significance to the individual as somehow transcending his social milieu in virtue of his uniquely personal subjectivity. Moreover, in view of its unqualified naturalistic basis there is certainly no scope whatsoever in this conception for attributing to the individual a personal relationship to a transcendent divine principle or a personal destiny transcending his historical existence. As envisaged by Marx communism provides a complete and self-sufficient solution to all the problems of human life and history. 'Communism as a fully developed naturalism is humanism and as a fully developed humanism is naturalism.

It is the *definitive* resolution of the antagonism between man and nature, and between man and man. It is the true solution of the conflict between existence and essence, between objectification and self-affirmation, between freedom and necessity, between individual and species. It is the solution of the riddle of history and knows itself to be this solution.'[25]

Thus Marx would argue that his scientific account of how a state of secular society can be achieved which will be totally adequate to human requirements provides a justification in principle of his humanist critique of religion as intrinsically alienating. This justification of an atheistic standpoint will have its *de facto* empirical verification through the revolutionary praxis, which will bring about the concrete realisation of the communist society. In virtue of his concrete accomplishment of this society man will have eradicated the conditions of the possibility of religion. For he will have overcome the economic alienation which is its hidden source and, in the process, will have provided himself with palpable evidence that his whole human reality and value has derived from within his own productive resources. Even the indirect reference to God, which characterises the conventional understanding of atheism, will no longer be necessary. As Marx himself puts it in the following extended quotation which might be said to summarise his entire philosophy of religion:

Since, however, for socialist man, the *whole of what is called world history* is nothing but the creation of man by human labour, and the emergence of nature for man, he, therefore, has the evident and irrefutable proof of his *self-creation*, of his own *origins*. Once the essence of man and of nature, man as a natural being and nature as a human reality, has become evident in practical life, in sense experience, the quest for an *alien* being, a being above man and nature (a quest which is the avowal of the unreality of man and nature) becomes impossible in practice. *Atheism,* as a denial of this unreality, is no longer meaningful, for atheism is a *negation of God* and seeks to assert by this negation the *existence of man*. Socialism no longer requires such a roundabout method; it begins from the *theoretical* and *practical sense perception* of man and nature as essential beings. It is positive human *self-consciousness,* no longer a self-consciousness attained through the negation of religion.[26]

Marx's thought represents an impressive attempt to ground in exclusively finite and secular terms the affirmation of an absolute meaning and value for human existence. We have seen how it adduces a conception of a totally fulfilled and integrated humanity as the verification in principle of the critique of a religious interpretation of reality. Moreover, Marx would have repudiated the charge, which he admitted could be levelled against Feuerbach, that the anticipated godless society of the communist era was merely wishful thinking. He would have insisted that it is a scientifically grounded prediction which discloses how man, if he chooses the requisite revolutionary means, can literally make himself totally self-sufficient. He would insist that he is proposing neither a utopian ideal nor a lifeless inevitability but rather a practical proposition challenging man to a course of action through which he can eradicate all alienation and make himself absolutely adequate to his needs and aspirations. Thus it might be said that his conception of communist man is an example not of wishful thinking but rather of dynamic wilful thinking. It is proposed as a well-founded self-transcending vision of a new kind of humanity as the goal and inspiration of committed historical endeavour. 'History will produce it, and the development which we already recognise in thought as self-transcending will in reality involve a severe and protracted process. We must consider it an advance, however, that we have previously acquired an awareness of the limited nature and the goal of the historical development and can see beyond it.'[27]

Notwithstanding the profound character of the atheism inherent in the Marxist viewpoint certain objections can be advanced against it. For example, it might be objected that the circuit of argument which sustains the affirmation of atheism remains essentially inconclusive inasmuch as the *de facto* confirmation of the critique of religion is located in the *future* realisation of an autonomous and religionless human condition. In other words, the contention that religion must be intrinsically alienating because humanity can achieve an integrated condition in which its non-reality *will be* empirically confirmed leaves the accuracy of this appraisal of religion to the future. Nevertheless its accuracy must be assumed as a necessary prerequisite of the praxis which will allegedly accomplish the empirical withering away of religion. For this accomplishment presupposes that man must 'revolve around himself as around his true sun' and orientate his action from within an exclusively socio-economic horizon. Thus what seems to be involved instead of conclusive argument is a *commitment* to making history unfold in the manner in which it must if the assumption of a totally immanent accomplishment of human autonomy is to be made good. That such autonomy and fulfilment are effectively within the resources of history, which in Marxist terms means the resources of human work, remains decidedly problematical.

It would remain problematical even if one granted Marx's allegedly scientific prediction that 'the severe and protracted process' involved in creating the communist society will surmount the concomitant hazards and contingencies and finally attain its goal. For it is not evident that even in such a society man would experience himself as adequately fulfilled and liberated from all alienation. Admittedly if man should so experience himself in a communist society, Marx's humanist theory of man is a plausible account of why this would be so. Indeed this theory might even be defended as a prescriptive account of how man might bring about a state of humanity in which the hypothesis of his complete auto-

GOD & ATHEISM - 211.8

GOD IS DEAD - 200.1

ATHEISM & LIBERATION 211.8

Alliance Leicester COMMERCIAL BANK

Name of Payer	Reference	Account Num
	Customer	
	Account Number	
	Cheque No.	

GRAND TOTAL - To be ente

fulfilment could be empirically tested. However, it is not itself a proof that this hypothesis will necessarily be verified. Marx's assurance that it will rests upon a questionable claim to have raised his head above history and apprehended in advance the absolute empirical outcome of the historical process.

More directly, various positive considerations can be adduced which challenge the contention that a communist society would in fact constitute empirical verification of complete human fulfilment and an effective elimination of the problem of God. It might be argued, for example, that this conception involves a restrictive view of man which considers him only in his dimensions of exteriority and social existence. As such it fails to come to grips with or satisfy the exigencies of inner personal authenticity upon which contemporary philosophy lays such emphasis.

Thus it might be pointed out that there is within each individual a genuine challenge to ascertain and to rise to the full truth of his own innermost subjectivity. This challenge to accomplish a project of fundamental self-knowledge and personal authenticity is not satisfied merely by rectifying the socio-economic maladjustments between men. For what is involved is a vertical dimension of internal equanimity rather than the horizontal dimension of social harmony. It can be objected that the Marxist conception of man fails to illuminate this ethical drama of interiority which, although not incompatible with the ethical drama of exteriority and society, is certainly not reducible to it. In brief, even granted the communist society, it is arguable that man will still be a problem to himself, potentially alienated and unfulfilled in his personal selfhood. To admit this, even as a possibility, constitutes a genuine objection to Marx's contention that with the advent of the communist society the elimination of all human alienation is assured and with it the eradication of the problem of God from human consciousness.[28]

As has already been suggested, the Marxist reply to this objection would be that in a fully socialised milieu the individual will appreciate the exclusively social significance of his own existence and will therefore simply not raise the question of his own personal trans-social meaning and value. At least if he does raise it, it will be merely in order to dismiss it at once as a pseudo-question.

However, many would argue that this merely defines a genuine area of human enquiry and discussion out of existence by insisting on an inadequate and ultimately incoherent account of the exclusively social significance of human existence. In other words it would be argued that it mistakenly assumes that because all human actions can in some respects be described as social they must be so in every respect.[29] This is incompatible with the point, acknowledged by Marx himself, that there is no social action which is not the action of individuals.[30] All social existence and action is the work of individual persons. As such it has an irreducibly 'first person singular' quality and consequently its significance cannot be exclusively social.

An individual subject, even of admittedly social activity, cannot be fully accounted for simply as a determinate set of social relationships within the comprehensive ongoing network of such relationships which constitute the course of the history of humanity. Unlike, for example, a figure in the game of chess, questions concerning the significance of the individual person cannot be adequately posed or answered in terms of the moves to be made or the relationships to be entered into with other individuals. For the individual person is, as Marx admits, 'the subjective existence of society as thought and experienced'.[31] Precisely as the conscious subject of the network of social relationships which characterise his involvement in the species life of humanity, each individual person encounters the problem of the ultimate significance of his own incommunicable subjectivity. However well adjusted and adequate the organisation of society to the exigencies of his social reality, it discloses no meaningful ground of this unique subjectivity through which he is inserted into the reality of ongoing community life and through which he lives the species life in a manner exclusively his own.

The individual person, precisely as conscious subject of community life, stands in a relationship of tangency to this community life and does not coincide absolutely with it. The meaning of his life (and indeed of his death), inasmuch as it is his own, cannot be adequately explicated in terms of the meaning of the life of the community. The content which is available to the individual through his participation in the historical community is incapable of fulfilling the kind of destiny and transcendence to which he might, at least conceivably, aspire.[32] Hence, it would appear that even under the most authentic socio-economic conditions, the individual will retain an exigency for trans-social personal authenticity. Even in a community of truth and justice in which the mutual recognition of man by man has been achieved, it does not seem reasonable to assume that discussion of an abiding personal destiny and the problem of God generally would disappear from human consciousness. To suggest, as Marx does, that it would presupposes a remarkable evolution of self-forgetfulness which is scarcely likely or desirable.

These reflections, which will be more fully developed later, should not obscure recognition of the considerable significance and influence of Marx's atheism. It represents a profound and in many respects inspiring project for the definitive resolution of human alienation. Its repudiation of a divine absolute is integrated into the wider context of an optimistic and practical vision of human destiny. Thus the reality of an absolute is emphatically reaffirmed in an exclusively secular form. The whole course of nature and human endeavour is seen as leading to the assured auto-constitution of humanity as an abiding and self-sufficient rational reality.

By substituting an 'absolute' human community for a transcendent divine absolute, Marxism claims to fulfil the deepest aspiration of modern thought. It claims to accomplish the complete coincidence of a thoroughgoing humanism of liberty and a universally acknowledged order of absolute truth and value. This conception of a totally immanent absolute, which is nothing other than humanity's complete and self-sufficient realisation of itself, represents an impressive theoretical and moral ideal. It is perhaps not so surprising that, in comparison with the intrinsically valuable activity of participating in the realisation of this autonomous humanity, Marxists consider questions concerning the personal destiny of the individual as such to be insignificant and even irrelevant. At all events, any contemporary theistic interpretation of the absolute and of human fulfilment must reckon seriously with this absolute humanism of Marx which still commends itself to so many people as a more authentic appraisal of reality.

6

Brave New World of Positivistic Naturalism

T H I S and the following chapter are not primarily concerned with presenting the thought of individual philosophers. They are rather an attempt to mediate a basic understanding of two of the most characteristic forms in which contemporary atheism finds expression, namely, existentialism and positivistic naturalism. Chapter seven is devoted to a discussion of existentialism. The present chapter confines itself to a consideration of positivistic naturalism.

Various nuances of the rather vague and cumbersome term 'positivistic naturalism' will be elucidated in the course of the following discussion. However, by way of preliminary description it may be said to connote the view according to which there is neither any basis nor any need to go beyond the world of experience and scientific explanation for an ultimate account of the meaning and value of reality in general and of human existence in particular.

This view draws its inspiration from many sources. Some of these have already been noted in previous chapters. For example, we have seen how the scientific revolution of the sixteenth and seventeenth centuries set afoot a new ideal of a purely immanentistic understanding of the world. It also made accessible to man an unprecedented control over nature and his own destiny with ever more remarkable consequences which tend to confine his interests and aspirations within an exclusively secular context. Similarly,

99

we have noted the profound impact of Kant's philosophy. We have seen how it restricted scientific knowledge of reality to that afforded by physical science and dismissed as illusory all metaphysical claims to provide knowledge of any reality transcending the bounds of experience.

Another source of positivistic naturalism which should be mentioned is the philosophical empiricism which has been the predominant influence in British philosophy since the seventeenth century. Likewise, account should be taken of the important current of eighteenth-century French materialism.

One could dwell upon various themes as crucial to the development of classical British empiricism. For example, one might consider certain aspects of the thought of Thomas Hobbes (1588–1679) who generalised the new scientific viewpoint into a philosophical mechanistic materialism. Or one might highlight John Locke's (1632–1704) insistence that the human mind is initially a *tabula rasa* and that all our knowledge originates in and from atomic sense impressions. Or again one might point out how George Berkeley (1685–1753) destroyed the tenuous and unjustified claim of Locke's empiricism to have maintained a bond between the ideas of experience and a divinely created external material world. However, all such reflections would only be anticipations of the philosophy of David Hume (1711–1776) in which classical empiricism found its fully mature expression and in which the essential philosophical ingredients of subsequent positivistic naturalism are laid down.

The relevant features of Hume's view on the problem of God are implied in his general methodological maxim: 'When we entertain, therefore, any suspicion that a philosophical term is employed without any meaning or idea (as is but too frequent), we need but enquire, *from what impression is that supposed idea derived?* And if it be impossible to assign any, this will serve to confirm our suspicion.'[1] According to Hume there can be no philosophical justification for the affirmation of any reality transcending the field of sense experience. In particular, his reformulation of the principle of causality in terms of a psychological habit of expectation arising from constantly associated ideas precludes the speculative transition from the data of sense experience to God as their transcendent cause.

Thus Hume relegates the whole question of the existence of God to the ambiguous realm of belief and argues that scepticism is the only philosophically viable position concerning the claims of reason to prove His existence. For example, in his *Dialogues Concerning Natural Religion* he discounts the claims of the design argument on the grounds that it rests upon inconclusive analogical reasoning. Further, he maintains that although a selective appeal to some aspects of experience, such as evidence of order in nature, suggests an affirmation of God based upon loose analogical comparison with human intelligence, other aspects of experience, such as evidence of disorder and evil, count against this affirmation. Hence, in Hume's estimation the most responsible attitude of reason is one which declines to accept as philosophically compelling the claim that one must go beyond the world of experience for an explanation of the phenomena of this world. We shall consider presently how this view is reiterated in a more explicit and emphatic form in contemporary positivistic naturalism.

Eighteenth-century French philosophy, which was considerably influenced by the views of British empiricists, was characterised by a tendency to absolutise the outlook of positive science. It was the philosophy of an age which looked to the progress of science for 'enlightenment' and reconciliation between men and it was ill-disposed to the 'dogmatic' claims of metaphysics which had enjoyed such favour during the preceding century.

Admittedly, in their attitude to the problem of God many of the great eighteenth-century thinkers such as Fontenelle (1657–1757), Montesquieu (1689–1757), Voltaire (1694–1778), Condillac (1715–1780) and the early Diderot (1713–1784) tended towards deism rather than atheism.

H

They acknowledged the existence of a supreme being and endorsed the value of natural religion. But they were uncompromising in their critique of all revealed and historical religions. They were convinced that the findings of natural science and the promptings of a moral code common to all men provided the only reliable guide to religious authenticity.

However, this era of French philosophy also included some notable materialist philosophers whose teaching was inherently atheistic such as La Mettrie (1709–1751), d'Holbach (1723–1789), and Cabanis (1757–1804). Their chief endeavour was a repudiation of all ultimate dualism, e.g. the dualism of body and soul and the dualism of God and nature. Descartes' description of the living body as a machine was taken as an adequate basis from which to account for the whole man, and the independent spiritual soul was dismissed as an unnecessary hypothesis. Likewise, their conception of nature as a self-determined and self-sustaining system of matter in which motion was an intrinsic property dispensed with the need for postulating God as the cause of motion or order. Hence, any appeal to God was rejected as philosophically irrelevant and even a source of delusion and human estrangement.[2]

These general remarks are obviously inadequate to the rich variety of views which found expression in eighteenth-century French thought. However, they do provide some indication of the predominantly secular mentality which characterised the age. Thus, in view of its widespread commitment to the method of science, its distrust of revealed religion and its strong current of strict materialism, one may certainly agree with Copleston's appraisal that 'the philosophy of the eighteenth century helped to prepare the way for the positivism of the following century.'[3]

The great apostle of nineteenth-century positivism was the French philosopher, Auguste Comte (1795–1857). It is noteworthy that the publication of his principal work, the

six-volume *Course of Positive Philosophy*, was completed in
1842, the year after the publication of Feuerbach's *The
Essence of Christianity*. Their influence, together with that of
Marx's historical materialism and the evolutionism of
Darwin (1809–1882), Huxley (1825–1895) and Spencer
(1820–1903), combined to mould the spirit of positivistic
naturalism which characterised the latter half of nineteenth-
century European culture.

The central theme of Comte's philosophy is his famous 'law
of the three states'. According to this fundamental doctrine,
all speculation on every subject of human enquiry must, both
in the case of each individual and in the race as a whole, pass
successively through three different theoretical states. These
are: 1) the theological; 2) the metaphysical; and 3) the
positive.

In its most primitive state, almost wholly dependent upon
feeling and imagination, human speculation takes a theological shape. In this theological state, which Comte also
calls the 'fictitious state', the human mind seeks to explain
all natural phenomena as though they were produced by the
immediate action of a supernatural being or beings.

The second or metaphysical state is a necessary but
ambiguous intermediary between the imaginative extrava-
gances of the first and the scientific rationality of the third.
In this metaphysical state the human mind seeks to explain
the inner nature and origin of all things by substituting for
the supernatural causes of theology the abstract and in
principle unobservable entities and categories of ontology.
Although in this metaphysical state the mind has pro-
gressed from seeking transcendent supernatural causes to
seeking explanatory principles inherent in nature itself its
achievement is at best merely a restatement of the observed
phenomena in abstract and mystifying terminology.

In its third, the positive state, 'the mind has given over the
vain search for Absolute notions, the origin and destination
of the universe, and the causes of phenomena, and applies
itself to the study of their laws,—that is, their invariable

relations of succession and resemblance. Reasoning and observation, duly combined, are the means of this knowledge. What is now understood when we speak of an explanation of facts is simply the establishment of a connection between single phenomena and some general facts, the number of which continually diminishes with the progress of science.'[4] The characteristic feature of this positive state is that all explanations must be in terms of what can be observed. It ignores all futile speculation concerning transcendent or even immanent metaphysical causes. It is concerned simply, after the manner of physical science, with establishing empirically verifiable natural laws concerning regular sequences of events. An absolute method, the method of science, replaces the absolute entities of theology and metaphysics.[5] Thus from the viewpoint of positive philosophy even metaphysical conceptions, such as Spinoza's absolute substance or Hegel's absolute spirit, which claimed to demythologise the theistic absolute of traditional theology, must themselves be demythologised and give way to the strictly empirical outlook of positive science.

In Comte's estimation the positive approach had already superseded theology and metaphysics in the study of every domain of natural phenomena. But it had not yet been brought to bear upon the field of social phenomena. Hence, the only outstanding requirement was to fill this one gap in the positive philosophy by establishing a 'social physics' which would extend the method of positive science to the study of social phenomena. When this has been achieved and all fundamental conceptions have become homogeneous the positive state would be fully and definitively established. 'It can never again change its character, though it will be forever in course of development by additions of new knowledge. Having acquired the character of universality which has hitherto been the only advantage resting with the two preceding systems, it will supersede them by its natural superiority, and leave to them only an historical existence.'[6] Once fully established, the positive philosophy will serve as a universal instrument of social harmony, prosperity and happiness.

Comte's positivism is in line with the optimistic appraisal of human destiny which, as we have seen, characterises other forms of nineteenth-century atheism such as those proposed by Feuerbach and Marx. He sees the positive philosophy, when successfully extended to embrace all social phenomena, as forming the basis of a new and pure religion consisting in the worship of Humanity. Rescued from the fears and illusions of theology and metaphysics by a scientific habit of thought which assures mankind of indefinite progress and which promotes the growth of brotherly love, all men will come to worship as the supreme being the sacred Humanity in which they participate.[7] The earnestness with which Comte dedicated himself in the latter part of his career to elaborating details of the cult, organisation and propagation of this new religion of Humanity, of which he himself was the self-appointed pontiff, is one of the more bizarre episodes of nineteenth-century cultural endeavour.[8]

Today the messianic optimism in which Comte's positive philosophy culminates must strike one as a somewhat utopian enthusiasm and as quite inappropriate to the complexities, hazards and moral ambiguities which are inherent in a scientific and technologically orientated culture. Similarly, there is a considerable over-simplification involved in his fundamental law of the three states according to which in the development of the human mind positive science must supersede and eliminate the theological and metaphysical modes of thought. For it is arguable that these represent three different but compatible points of view from which a subject can consider the realities of his experience. Thus it might be argued that through the evolution and differentiation of their distinctive methodologies we can come to a purified understanding at all three levels rather than to the inevitable elimination of two of them as obsolete. As de Lubac remarks: 'If, then, it is true to say that "physics" (in the sense of the whole of science) began by being theological, it would be just as true to say that theology began by being physical, and the law of evolution does not tend to expel theology any more than science, but to "purify" both by differentiating them.'[9] In other words, the primitiveness of earlier speculation consisted in its confusion of different disciplines, not simply in its tendency to 'mystify' nature. Further, as will be seen in chapter seven, one of the most striking features of contemporary existentialist philosophy is its rebuttal of the attempt of Comte's kind of 'scientism' to restrict all valid knowledge, particularly about man, to that obtained through the method of positive science.

Nevertheless, whatever its shortcomings, Comte's positivism represents one of the most detailed and important attempts to articulate the case for a naturalistic outlook inspired by the theory and practice of modern science. The attraction of such an outlook has exercised, and continues to exercise, a considerable influence upon the thought of the present century. In ordinary consciousness this outlook assumes the form of a scientific humanism which expects from the marvels of science a resolution of all man's problems, anxieties and needs. In its philosophical expression it tends to confine itself chiefly to resisting resolutely any appeal to a non-empirical or transcendent explanation of the world. This twentieth-century positivistic naturalism, which avoids the optimistic exuberance of Comte's 'religious' positivism and is more in the spirit of the prudent scepticism of classical empiricism, could be illustrated in various philosophical contexts. For example, it finds expression in the American strand of scientific empiricism typified by the philosophy of John Dewey (1859–1952).[10] Likewise, certain versions of contemporary structuralist philosophy, notably that developed by Claude Lévi-Strauss, are essentially refined forms of neo-positivism.[11] However, in the following pages, we shall limit our discussion of contemporary positivistic naturalism to its manifestation in certain aspects of twentieth-century British philosophy.

A unifying bond underlying the considerable variety and developments of twentieth-century British philosophy is its conviction that the primary task of philosophy is not the exploration and discovery of new empirical or transcendent realities but rather the analysis of the meaning of language. It seeks to elucidate the various ways in which language accomplishes significant communication. Concomitantly it provides an account of how and why language may fail to accomplish significant communication, particularly in those cases where this failure is not immediately evident. It is this latter consideration, when directed to an analysis of language about God, which sustains the strand of positivistic naturalism in contemporary British philosophy.[12]

The most uncompromising form in which this naturalism has found expression is in the philosophy of logical positivism which enjoyed particular notoriety earlier in the century. According to logical positivism, human discourse is either a) emotive or b) cognitive. Emotive discourse is factually uninformative. It serves merely to express or arouse feeling or to stimulate to action. The function of cognitive discourse is the communication of informative statements. In its analysis of cognitive discourse logical positivism maintains that apart from analytic statements, which are mere tautologies or linguistic conventions, the only meaningful class of statements are those factual statements which are verifiable in terms of sense experience. Thus, according to the famous principle of verification, as defended, for example, by A. J. Ayer in his *Language, Truth and Logic*, the meaning of any allegedly factual statement consists in the method whereby it might be empirically verified.[13] If no experience relevant to its verification can be adduced it is, strictly speaking, neither true nor false but quite literally meaningless. Moreover, in order to be deemed meaningful it must not involve as part of its proposed meaning anything that cannot be represented as an observation statement.

In the light of this theory of meaning, the affirmation of the existence of God and theological statements generally are numbered amongst the statements which are to be dismissed as meaningless. If, for example, the statement 'There is a transcendent God' is to be counted as meaningful it must be possible to deduce from it, or at least from it and other empirical hypotheses, certain observation statements which are not deducible from these other hypotheses alone. Certain factual statements might be thought to fulfil this condition, e.g. those statements relating to the order manifested in nature by phenomena such as the regular succession of the seasons and the organised development of plant and animal life. These, it might be thought, could be taken as relevant empirical evidence for the affirmation of the existence of God. But in fact, the logical positivist would argue, whereas such observation statements about seasons and living beings might be taken as tending to confirm assertions about a certain order in nature, they have no crucial bearing upon the fundamental feature of the affirmation of God, namely, His existence as the *transcendent* being whose being is not reducible without residue to His empirical manifestations. Thus Ayer remarks: 'If the sentence "God exists" entails no more than that certain types of phenomena occur in certain sequences, then to assert the existence of a god will be simply equivalent to asserting that there is the requisite regularity in nature; and no religious man would admit that this was all he intended to assert in asserting the existence of a god.'[14] Inasmuch as the affirmation of God's existence necessarily involves as part of its proposed meaning the metaphysical feature of transcendence, which cannot be empirically represented, it fails to assert anything which might be either true or false. It is simply nonsensical.

Similarly, by the logical positivist criterion of meaning, all statements concerning mystical intuitions, visions and miracles are to be dismissed as meaningless. For the experiences which are adduced as relevant to their verification are inadequate to support the supernatural significance alleged in such statements. The mystic's description of a vision merely gives us indirect information about the condition of his mind. Likewise, unless one resorts to the question-begging device of introducing the supernatural into the definition of events, one cannot logically exclude the possibility of a simply natural explanation of the events which are adduced as empirical evidence for the assertion of a miracle. Thus no crucially relevant empirical evidence can be indicated whereby the truth or even the falsity of statements about the supernatural might be tested.

Ayer, with characteristic directness, summarises the logical positivist view of all theistic assertions when he declares that 'they are merely providing material for the psycho-analyst'.[15] Failing to issue in the kind of empirically verifiable propositions which constitute science, the theist's claims to factual knowledge can be dismissed as exercises in self-deception.

Thus logical positivism, by insisting that the only authentic form of factual knowledge is that which is empirically verifiable, reiterates the naturalistic thesis that theological and metaphysical speculation is, in principle, inauthentic, mystifying and dehumanising. Since such speculation is not simply inadequate or false but quite literally meaningless, the man who seeks to explain himself and his world in terms of God alienates whatever meaning and value he might have by grounding them in a context of meaningless chatter.

In the development of linguistic philosophy over the past quarter of a century logical positivism has been severely criticised and superseded by more refined theories of meaning.[16] For example, the point has often been made that its absolute criterion of meaningfulness, the principle of verification, is even by its own standard meaningless or at least quite unsuitable as an absolute standard of meaningfulness. For if, as would seem to be the most plausible interpretation, it claims to be making a factual assertion that the meaning of every significant statement consists either in a tautological linguistic convention or a factual assertion referring to relevant sense experiences, this assertion is itself unverifiable by relevant sense experiences. There are no such sense experiences as could confirm assertions about the logical significance of all statements. If on the other hand the principle is interpreted as an analytic statement defining the usage of the term 'meaningful statement' it cannot preclude the adoption of alternative definitions of 'meaningful statement'. Nor is the dilemma avoided by the suggestion that the principle is neither a tautology nor a statement of empirical fact but simply a *recommendation* that we treat as meaningful only tautologies and empirical statements. For an analysis of the nature of tautologies and empirical statements yields no refutation of the objection that any such recommendation is arbitrary and logically uncompelling.

More directly, it has been argued that logical positivism unjustifiably generalises the verification principle from its limited function of deciding whether or not any given statement is empirically informative to judging the meaningfulness of every dimension of discourse. It subordinates all human discourse to the traditional empiricist assumptions: a) that knowledge is ultimately limited to sense impressions; b) that what makes language meaningful is its correspondence with those sense impressions by which it may be ostensively defined. These assumptions have influenced logical positivism to treat the factually informative statements of science as the standard of all meaningful discourse and to restrict its understanding of factually informative statements to the context of the experientially verifiable. Hence, its rejection of all theological and metaphysical discourse as nonsense is fundamentally a rejection of it in terms of a framework of assumptions concerning knowledge and meaning from which acceptance of such discourse is by definition excluded.

Present-day linguistic philosophy no longer accepts these empiricist assumptions concerning knowledge and meaning as completely or at least as explicitly as did logical positivism. Even if, as we shall see, there is reason to believe that their influence is still effective beneath the surface it is so in an unthematised and less belligerent manner. In its current form linguistic philosophy favours a more flexible and less iconoclastic conception of meaning. One of the chief sources of inspiration of this more recent approach to meaning was the Austrian philosopher, Ludwig Wittgenstein (1889–1951), who taught at Cambridge and is generally acknowledged as the most important and influential philosopher of the age. In his *Philosophical Investigations* he emphasises that there are many genuinely meaningful kinds of human discourse, each with its own distinctive logical structure, and that it is inadmissible to treat the statements of science as the privileged criterion of all meaningful discourse. Thus, language functions quite meaningfully not merely in communicating analytic definitions and empirically informative facts but also, for example, in issuing commands, making pledges, evaluating events, evoking responses, acknowledging favours and expressing feelings.[17] Hence, the meaningfulness of expressions should be gauged not simply by reference to relevant sense experience but, more comprehensively, by a consideration of their successful use in a given context of discourse. Philosophical questions about the meaningfulness of various expressions are conducted by paying close attention to how they make sense as used in their typical settings whether these be everyday, poetic or technical. For example, the meaningfulness of an expression such as: 'Trailing clouds of glory do we come/From God Who is our home.' would be evaluated not in terms of relevant empirical evidence but in terms of how it functions effectively in the poetic usage of language. Thus the slogan which summarises the orientation of contemporary linguistic philosophy is that *the meaning of language is found in its use.*

In view of this more flexible conception of meaning, present-day linguistic philosophy is more favourably disposed than was logical positivism towards theological and metaphysical language about God. Such language is no longer dismissed automatically as in principle meaningless.

On the contrary careful attention is paid to the manner in which the theologian uses his language to develop a theological universe of discourse. Moreover, various techniques of linguistic analysis have been fruitfully applied in corroboration of theistic assertions.[18]

Nevertheless, the development of linguistic philosophy has by no means tended uniformly to support a theistic viewpoint. For example, even the willingness to treat theological language as meaningful, in some cases appears to be based exclusively on considerations of the internal logical coherence of this language and at the price of prescinding from all discussion of whether or not anything real corresponds to this universe of discourse. Thus the meaningfulness of language about God is reaffirmed in a way which relativises the significance of His real existence. This involves a subtle displacement of the basic intention of theology itself which envisages itself as expressing objective truths about God. To suppose that, provided theological language can be used in a coherent manner, the question of God's existence is incidental to its meaningfulness has a trivialising effect upon the seriousness of purpose of theological enquiry. As Donald Evans remarks: 'Questions of theological truth are not replaceable by questions concerning the internal logical "grammar" of biblical language.'[19]

Moreover, the willingness of contemporary linguistic philosophy to undertake an openminded investigation of theological language as a possible area of meaningful discourse has by no means led to universal agreement that it is in fact meaningful. Indeed on various points arguments have been advanced to maintain that on examination such language turns out to be meaningless. It is argued that it involves all sorts of confusion such as: a) employing incompatible uses of terminology; b) hopelessly muddling the meaning of terms by using them in a sense quite alien to their typical or paradigm usage; and c) evacuating terms of any clearly assignable meaning whatsoever. In other words, the theist's claim to be using language meaningfully, having been given a fair hearing, is found to be wanting.

An instance of theology's alleged employment of incompatible uses of terminology is its use of both concrete and abstract terms to designate the divine perfection. For example, we say both that 'God is good' and that 'God is goodness'. Thus in respect of these predicates the term 'God' is made to function both as a concrete or common noun and as an abstract noun. To this it has been objected that: 'We cannot have it both ways, and use a word as an abstract noun and a common noun at once, as you try to do in your sentence "God is his own goodness"—that's just bad grammar, a combining of words which fails to make them mean —like "Cat no six". . . . This word [God] as you use it, does not and cannot name anything whatever—you refuse to put it through the proper motions of "naming".'[20]

Similarly, arguments have been advanced to maintain that much of the language about God involves an unjustified transposition of terms from the context which determines their standard or typical usage. The description of God as a necessary being is frequently adduced as a clear example of such a linguistic muddle or 'category mistake'. It is argued that since necessity is a property of statements and not of things, and since the term 'necessary' signifies simply and exclusively a property of those formally valid statements which are in principle factually uninformative, it is, therefore, not merely false but actually meaningless to affirm the existence of God as necessary being. 'For the distinction between necessity and contingency is not a distinction between different sorts of entities, but between different sorts of statement. . . . This is the only use of them which does not give rise to impossible difficulties.'[21]

Finally, it is commonly argued that theological statements are devoid of meaning because in refusing to admit that anything could falsify them they are equivalently failing to assert anything. This argument expresses a principle, namely, the falsification principle, which is obviously related to the verification principle of logical positivism. According to this falsification principle, a statement is meaningless if it is impossible to specify a state of affairs which would count against or be incompatible with its truth. This principle is applied to statements such as: 'God loves us'; 'God is good'; 'God is an almighty provident creator'. Thus, for example, if the theist can allow no conceivable eventuality, however reprehensible, to count against his statement that God is a loving provident Father, he is not really asserting anything meaningful in thus describing God. For, although such an utterance appears *prima facie* to assert the actuality of a particular state of affairs, it fails to mark out the state of affairs inasmuch as it is allegedly compatible with every possible state of affairs. It thus fails to fulfil the conditions of being a genuine or meaningful statement at all.[22]

These sorts of arguments against the meaningfulness of language about God have not been left unconsidered by either traditional or contemporary theistic philosophers. For example, St Thomas Aquinas devoted particular attention to the apparent conflict in the use of both concrete and abstract terms to describe the divine perfection. He argued that in human discourse the abstract and the concrete uses of a term have a profoundly different significance. The concrete use can signify a complete, actually subsistent, individual being, but always involves a connotation of composition and consequently of finitude. The abstract use can abstract from this implication of finitude but only by introducing a connotation of non-subsistence or non-actuality. In describing the objects of our experience we can distinguish adequately between these two uses. Further, we can indicate a basis for the distinction in the composite character of material beings and in our intellectual capacity to consider concrete principles in an abstract way. However, when attempting to speak about a divine perfection which transcends our direct or proper comprehension, which undoubtedly subsists but is also undoubtedly not finite, we realise the inadequacy of either abstract or concrete terms to represent such a perfection. It is precisely because of this inadequacy of either abstract or concrete terms to represent properly the divine perfection which they both signify that both can be predicated of God notwithstanding their seeming incongruity. For each compensates an aspect of the inadequacy of the other.[23]

Aquinas would argue, therefore, that an account of the divine perfection will inevitably appear to involve bad grammar and a violation of the syntax of our language. For language, as a symbolic formulation of our knowledge, is determined in its articulation by the limitations proper to our way of knowing. And, therefore, since we can know the divine infinite perfection only indirectly and inadequately, through reflection on our knowledge of the finite world, it is to be expected that the terminology by which we 'name' the divine perfection will involve us in certain anomalies and inadequacies. Indeed an infinite being which language could adequately name according to the norms appropriate to the denomination of finite beings would be a pseudo-infinite, a mere instance of a rule, subject to classification, and consequently de-transcendentalised.

It does not follow, however, that expedients such as the employment of both the concrete and the abstract uses of terms to describe the divine perfection are just wild talk. Because of our inability to represent such perfection adequately we seek to minimise this inadequacy by resorting to a linguistic device which would not be justified in the description of finite material being. However, we are aware of what we are doing and can provide an account of why we are doing it. Our exceptional linguistic usage is justified and controlled both by whatever reasoning led us to affirm that infinite being really exists as the transcendent source of all finite being, and by our knowledge that although we can formulate appropriate identifying references to this infinite being, nevertheless our manner of framing these references is inadequate to represent the objective perfection which they signify.[24]

Similarly, the argument that the description of God as

necessary being involves a distorted use of language has been criticised. It has been pointed out that the restriction of the meaningful use of the term 'necessary' to signify a property of propositions rather than of things is unduly selective.[25] It fails to take account of the historically accepted and coherent usage of the term to signify a being which cannot not be or, more specifically, in the case of God the self-sufficiency and eternity of the divine perfection. Hence, the claim that it is meaningless to speak about God as necessary being *because* necessity can only signify a property of propositions is not really a conclusion from the only coherent meaning of necessity but rather an indirect restatement of the Humean and Kantian contention that there could not *be* anything which necessarily is. To such a contention Professor Geach has pertinently replied that: 'Since what is "necessary" is what "cannot "not be, to say that "necessary" can only refer to logical necessity is equivalent to saying that whatever cannot be so, *logically* cannot be so—e.g. that since I cannot speak Russian, my speaking Russian is logically impossible: which is absurd.'[26]

Also, the argument that language about God such as describes Him as a loving provident Father is meaningless, because unverifiable, has been met in various ways. For example, writers such as Crombie, Hick and Copleston have suggested that one might accept the falsification theory of meaning but transfer the context of verification and falsific-ation to the next life. Thus 'God is a loving Father' should be understood in terms of the specific promise of heavenly beatitude and would preclude or be falsified by the truth of the statement 'God wishes the eternal damnation and misery of all human beings.'[27]

Others have argued that it is quite inappropriate to seek to test assertions such as 'God is a loving Father' by the principle of falsification. For such an assertion expresses, not an empirically describable and hence falsifiable state of affairs, but rather an unreserved though not irrational commitment to the trustworthiness of God based upon whatever evidence we have accepted that He exists and is such as to be worthy of our total commitment. 'In other words, one trusts ahead of time that everything will be under God's providence for one's good, without laying down any humanly conceived empirical conditions or tests by which His love will be judged.'[28] On this view, the insistence that the principle of falsification be applicable to all theological assertions rests upon the empiricist presumption that in the final analysis the only cognitive function of language is to convey specific experiential information. Such a presumption is seen as insensitive to the possibility that theological language may fulfil a genuinely cognitive function by promoting a global comprehension of reality as such, as distinct from scientific knowledge of particular regions of experience. This language, it would be argued, expresses the mind's recourse to certain ultimate and pervasive concepts which, although not empirically falsifiable, constitute an intellectually satisfying appraisal of the ultimate meaning and value of reality as a whole.

These objections of linguistic philosophers to theological discourse exemplify how, in a modified form, positivistic naturalism continues to exercise considerable influence in contemporary British philosophy. Undoubtedly the development of linguistic philosophy has achieved a more accommodating conception of meaning in terms of coherent usage than the logical positivist bluntly verificationist account. Nevertheless, the naturalistic presumption that there is nothing outside a self-sufficient natural order, all of whose varied forms and functions are intrinsically dependent upon matter, profoundly affects the contemporary conception of coherent usage. The widespread conviction persists that the range of coherent *cognitive* usage is confined within the manifold dimensions of empirically testable discourse about the internal organisation of the natural world. The difficulties which arise in trying to use our inherently worldly language to talk about God are seen as reinforcing the naturalistic presumption that nature is the limiting horizon of meaningful discourse. Hence, the possibility of providing a cogent proof for the existence of God as the transcendent source of the natural world is discounted. Similarly, language about God is treated as either fundamentally meaningless or, at best, an expression of non-cognitive emotions and attitudes.

This naturalistic presumption, which implicitly influences much of present-day linguistic philosophy about God, has been explicitly and unequivocally championed by Professor Flew in his book *God and Philosophy*. In this incisive work, which proposes to examine the case for Christian theism, he first of all advances the principal contemporary objections against the meaningfulness and even the morality of an affirmation of God. He then proceeds, in the course of a critique of the traditional proofs for God, to argue that it is inherently more rational to seek an explanation of reality in naturalistic rather than in theistic terms. We will conclude our discussion of the strand of positivistic naturalism in contemporary British philosophy with a brief consideration of this revealing illustration of it provided by Flew.

Following Hume he calls the principle which expresses his naturalism 'the Stratonician presumption' because it was first clearly formulated by Strato, next but one in succession to Aristotle as head of the Lyceum. Flew states his own version of the Stratonician presumption in the following terms: 'The presumption, defeasible of course by adverse argument, must be that all qualities observed in things are qualities belonging by natural right to those things themselves; and hence that whatever characteristics we think ourselves able to discern in the universe as a whole are the underivative characteristics of the universe itself.'[29]

There is a preliminary difficulty, which should perhaps be noted, concerning Flew's proclamation of the Stratonician presumption. He suggests that it must be presumed to be more rational to expect a final account of the qualities of the world in terms of its own intrinsic principles than to suppose that it may have been created by God. This suggestion is unwarranted. For the constraining force of such a presumption would depend upon the evidence which could be adduced in its defence. The only crucially relevant evidence would be that which is based upon an unprejudiced evaluation of the respective claims of both naturalism and theism. In other words, it is unreasonable to presume *a priori* that it is more rational to favour a naturalistic account of the world rather than to allow as equally possible, until the evidence decides, a theistic explanation. Indeed, if anything, it would seem to be more reasonable to presume that there may be a theistic explanation of the world than to presume that there is a naturalistic explanation. For such a presumption would be more impartial and would not exclude an eventual verdict in favour of naturalism in the way in which Flew's presumption tends to exclude an eventual verdict in favour of theism.

In fact, however, Flew does advance arguments in support of his naturalistic presumption, which he admits is in principle defeasible. His fundamental contention is that the alleged non-self-sufficiency of the world upon which the theist bases his affirmation of God could never be known by man, and that the available evidence points rather to a naturalistic explanation of the world. He applies this consideration to the argument from the order of nature to God as its intelligent designer.[30] He sees the crucial step in such an argument to be the assertion that the elements of the universe are of themselves diverse and exhibit no tendency to form a pattern. It is because this is so that God is invoked as the supra-mundane cause of their actual order.

Flew replies that we could never know what tendencies the elements of the world do or do not possess 'of themselves' as opposed to the way in which they do in fact behave under the conditions of their worldly context. For to obtain such knowledge one would have to be able to study the elements either in isolation from the world, which is absurd, and/or without the alleged influence of divine control—a project which the theist must exclude as impossible. Hence, instead of indulging in insoluble speculation about the limitations of the inherent tendencies of things, one should adopt the more straightforward view that the order manifested by the elements of the world is a natural, and therefore un-derived, property of these elements. This view is more rational than the supposition that the order in the universe which appears to obtain naturally cannot do so and must therefore arise through the agency of a supra-natural being.[31]

Flew proposes a similar defence of naturalism in his dis-cussion of various versions of the cosmological argument which attempts to explain finite conditioned existence in terms of an infinite unconditioned creator.[32] He sees such arguments as vitiated by an indefensible conception of explanation according to which it is an inherent defect of every naturalistic system that in any such system the most fundamental laws of matter and energy cannot be suscept-ible of any further explanation. It is supposed that a natural-istic explanation is inevitably imperfect because it must rest upon the acceptance of brute facts whereas this defect is remedied in a theistic system which, with its affirmation of God as necessary being, provides a sufficient reason to explain everything that happens.

Flew argues that the alleged defect is not a defect at all but a necessary truth about the nature of all explanation and that the appeal to God is not the privileged exception which it is thought to be. For explanation at every stage consists in showing how what is to be explained is an instance of or can be derived from a wider set of regularities, which at that stage has to be accepted as a brute fact. The ultimate explanation in any chain of explanation is itself inevitably something which must be accepted as an unexplained fact. 'Yet this is not, if the system is true, a defect; nor is it one which, even if theism were true, theism could remedy. For it is not a contingent fact about one sort of system, but a logical truth about all explanations of facts. The ultimate facts about God would have to be, for precisely the same reason, equally inexplicable.'[33] The illusory supposition that an appeal to God as logically necessary being could provide a sufficient reason or self-evident explanation for everything is, as Kant saw, merely a variation of the heart of the discredited ontological argument which seeks to decide by definition how existence must be.

Thus Flew rejects as incoherent the ideal of total explanation which he believes lends a superficial aura of plausibility to the affirmation of God. To allow the kind of contrast between contingent and necessary being which characterises the argument from contingency, is to envisage contingent beings as inherently deficient instances of being and thereby to undermine any ultimate explanation which remains at the level of such beings.[34] However, once it is appreciated that this alleged contrast between necessary and contingent being rests upon an indefensible ideal of explanation, the presumption in favour of an ultimate explanation of events in naturalistic terms will be seen to be undefeated. This is the contention which Flew reiterates in the closing sentences of his book: 'We therefore conclude, though as always subject to correction by further evidence and further argument, that the universe itself is ultimate; and, hence, that whatever science may from time to time hold to be the most fundamental laws of nature must, equally provisionally, be taken as the last words in any series of answers to questions as to why things are as they are. The principles of the world lie themselves "inside" the world.'[35]

A theist might take issue with various features of Flew's presentation and defence of the Stratonician presumption. For example, he might question the immediate inference, which is central to Flew's position, that the qualities observed in things in general and presumed to belong to them by natural right are therefore underived. Thus one critic points out that there are various contexts in which one commonly speaks of qualities belonging by natural right which are obviously derived qualities. For example, we are said to have a natural right to life even though our life has been derived from our parents.[36] More directly, a theist would want to argue that a theory of divine creation, as distinct from a doctrine of divine emanation, positively requires that the derived qualities of things in a created universe 'are qualities belonging by natural right to these things themselves'. For creation signifies a divine gift of total being which, though wholly from God, is also wholly other than God. In virtue of this gift of creation the recipient enjoys 'by natural right' its own proper existence and autonomous principles of operation. In brief, the theist would contest Flew's claim that 'underivative' is part of the meaning of 'belonging by natural right'.

Certain objections might also be urged against the defence of the Stratonician presumption which Flew elaborates in his critique of the arguments from order and contingency. For example, it might be objected that the argument from order does not depend, as Flew suggests, upon knowledge of how the ordered things of the world would behave in isolation from the world and/or divine control, but rather upon a metaphysical analysis of their *de facto* limited natural order considered in the light of our own experience of ordering. Moreover, the suggestion that since the universe is naturally ordered this order is underived is merely an application of the questionable tenet, discussed above, that 'underivative' is part of the meaning of 'belonging by natural right'. It does not follow that because things behave naturally in an orderly fashion, a creative source of such order is thereby precluded.

Similarly, the theist might contend that Flew's critique of the argument from contingency is based upon too restrictive an account of the nature of explanation. It presumes that the only coherent kind of explanation is one in terms of generalised natural laws. In thus presuming that every process of explanation must terminate at the level of unexplained fact it does not really meet the theistic contention that the proof for the existence of God establishes the truth of a wider conception of explanation. For the theist would argue that the proof establishes the existence of God as the ultimate explanation of contingent events in a manner which simultaneously establishes that He is His own *raison d'être*. The theist would therefore repudiate the presumption that a theistic explanation could not be superior to a naturalistic one because it too, like every explanation, would have to terminate in unexplained brute fact.

We need not pause at this point to expand and evaluate the theistic response to Flew's position.[37] For our immediate aim is simply to outline this position as a clear illustration of the positivistic naturalism which is both a significant strand in contemporary British philosophy and, more generally, a most influential and persistent source of contemporary atheism. Previous chapters have described the progressive development through modern thought of a reversal of the traditional theistic world-view. Here, in Flew's presentation of the Stratonician presumption, we find an explicit and revealing proclamation of the naturalistic version of this reversal.

As was indicated at the beginning of this study, the presumption of the traditional world-view, prior to the emergence of modern science and modern philosophy, was that a theistic explanation of the universe was the rational, indeed almost the self-evident, approach to an appraisal of reality. Objections which might be raised against such an appraisal were analysed as difficulties to be resolved through a refinement of theological and philosophical speculation. Such objections did not have the effect of causing people to question in a radical way the basic theistic presumption which provided the unquestioned context within which theological and philosophical speculation unfolded. Although positivistic naturalism involves a complete negation of this world-view it nevertheless shares a certain formal similarity with it. For it too, like the traditional position, involves a culturally conditioned presumption which predisposes it to treat objections as difficulties to be resolved within the context of a firmly accepted viewpoint rather than as calling in question the viewpoint itself.

The remarkable growth and achievements of empirical science underpin the naturalistic presumption that the material world, as amenable to the experimental method of science, defines the unified field of any rational appraisal of reality. The naturalistic and theistic viewpoints are not considered as alternatives which *prima facie* are equally plausible and whose respective claims must be evaluated impartially. On the contrary, naturalism is accepted as in rightful possession of the modern mind so that any contender must argue its claims in accordance with naturalistic criteria of meaningfulness. This requirement militates against a sympathetic reception of the case for theism which finds itself obliged to conform to conditions of rational discourse in which it cannot find adequate expression. Such, for example, is the situation in which theism finds itself from the standpoint of Flew's Stratonician atheism. This, having begun by accepting the presumption 'that the universe is everything there is; and hence that everything which can be explained must be explained by reference to what is in and of the universe', drew the obvious conclusion that 'Approaching the concept of God from this standpoint it appeared that there were very strong reasons for thinking it to be incoherent.'[38] It could scarcely have appeared otherwise since, from the standpoint adopted, an affirmation of God is by definition precluded.

Positivistic naturalism is a rejection of all theological, metaphysical and ideological absolutes. Yet it too can be considered as affirming an all-embracing absolute, namely, an absolutised method of scientific enquiry whose objective counterpart, the material world, is taken to be the absolute foundation of every form and function of reality. Thus considered, it can be seen as furthering the tendency of post-Hegelian thought to eradicate the unacceptable doctrine of absolute spirit by developing an exclusively and explicitly secular version of the unified conception of reality envisaged by that doctrine. To this extent it makes common cause with the absolute humanism defended, as we have seen, by thinkers such as Feuerbach and Marx.

On the other hand, positivistic naturalism, at least in its contemporary expression, represents a less optimistic form of atheism than that of Feuerbach and Marx. It is at one with these philosophers in affirming that belief in God is a profound source of human alienation. But it is less inclined to claim to have within its own resources the means of achieving a complete resolution of all human misery and alienation. Unlike its nineteenth-century Comtian counter-part it is not convinced that it is the assured source of continuous progress. Nor does it see itself as accomplishing some great destiny such as the religious veneration of scientific humanity. It confines its attestations to pointing out that in so far as human liberation and progress is attainable it is so only through irreversible commitment to nature as the totality of the real and to the logic of the sciences as the measure of rationality. Moreover, the evaluation of man exclusively in scientific terms has led, through the development of the sciences themselves, to an increasingly circumspect appraisal of his intrinsic significance and future prospects. This is so not only because of the practical repercussions of science in the form of environmental hazards and psychic pressures, but also in virtue of various theoretical insights achieved by the sciences themselves. For example, the expansion of astronomy has in a sense reduced the human milieu to insignificant cosmic proportions; the findings of the biological theory of evolution have highlighted the instability of our form of life and our temporal origin in the pre-rational world; and psychoanalytical research has disclosed the deep unconscious springs of our thought and action. Thus to some degree even the developments of science itself suggest certain reservations concerning the prospects of achieving the humanist ideal of complete scientific control of human action and natural processes.

Nevertheless, it would be misleading to maintain that

positivistic naturalism represents a fundamentally pessimistic view of man or that it is characterised by a sense of the absurdity of the human condition. If its basic presumption that 'the principles of the world lie exclusively within the world' is a source of metaphysical ennui it is also and more directly a summons to ever greater technological exploitation of the scientifically envisaged world. Its prevailing ethos is one which seeks to 'make good' its presumption that nature is all there is. This goal is promoted chiefly through the mediation of instruments which man fashions for himself to control the processes of nature. Thus man takes his destiny more and more into his own hands through the progressive transformation of his environment into an exosomatic milieu—i.e. into a technological prolongation of his body to be utilised rather than simply endured.[39] Indications that the complete accomplishment of this goal is an ever receding horizon, and even that the technological mediations through which man achieves greater control of nature can themselves constitute a new kind of danger for man, are not taken as reasons for despair. They are taken rather as challenges to renewed efforts of rationalisation. For irreversible commitment to science and technology is seen as leading along the only possible road to the concrete actualisation and expansion of human liberation which is the driving ideal of modern man. The extent to which this ideal is realisable is not prejudged metaphysically but left to the ongoing achievements of science and technology to disclose.

Thus positivistic naturalism as a scientific habit of mind, which precludes the metaphysical mode of thought, involves an atheism whose implications are calculated pragmatically rather than metaphysically. Its contraction of the range of significant discourse to within empirical boundaries, combined with its remarkable practical control of reality thus envisaged, favours an unconcerned forgetfulness of the problem of God rather than an agonising dwelling upon the consequences of His non-existence. It favours a practical humanism which it promotes as the rational implementation of a scientific outlook rather than as an ideological substitute for theism. For a more self-conscious and metaphysically orientated formulation of the significance and consequences of contemporary atheism we must direct our attention to the philosophy of existentialism.

7

Existentialism and the Rejection of Idols

EXISTENTIALISM, which is more a distinctive style of philosophising than a clearly defined philosophical doctrine, has found expression in a variety of forms. Some of these are theistic, notably the existentialism of S. Kierkegaard (1813–1855), K. Jaspers (1883–1969), and G. Marcel (1889–). Others are decidedly atheistic, for example, the existentialism of J. P. Sartre (1905–), M. Merleau-Ponty (1908–1961), and A. Camus (1923–1960). In this chapter we will consider some of the important features of the manner in which existentialist philosophy has been developed along atheistic lines. This consideration, it is hoped, will facilitate clearer insight into the overall significance of the evolution of contemporary atheism. Further, it will provide us with a point of departure from which, in our concluding chapter, we will indicate how a reappraisal of the problem of God might be undertaken today.

A characteristic feature of all existentialist philosophy, whether atheistic or otherwise, is that it unfolds from the standpoint of individual subjectivity. This signifies more than the banal truth that all philosophising is inevitably the work of an individual subject. It means that existentialism resists the common philosophical presumption that to know truly and profoundly we must achieve a transformation of consciousness from the standpoint of individual subjectivity to that of a detached impersonal spectator of an absolute order of objective reality. On the contrary it insists that only by consciously adopting and maintaining as basic and irreducible the phenomenological standpoint of concrete subjectivity can we have access to authentic philosophical truth. As we shall see, it is precisely through fidelity to a particular interpretation of the exigencies of this standpoint that various versions of existentialism have been led to an atheistic evaluation of reality.

The existentialist commitment to subjectivity must not be confused with philosophical subjectivism. It is not a glorification of arbitrariness or sheer relativism. It represents not a flight from reason but rather an attempt to achieve a more appropriate conception of human rationality. It seeks to show how each individual can come to an enriched self-awareness through personalised reflection upon the forms and dimensions of his own typically human experience as a subject incarnate in a world with other people.

A critique of both the materialism of positivistic naturalism and the intellectualism of transcendental idealism is involved in this basic standpoint of existentialism. It would argue that each of these philosophical alternatives represents a detotalisation of reality arising from an inadequate and one-sided consideration. It sees its own approach in terms of concrete subjectivity as a means of disclosing and overcoming this inadequacy of both positivism and idealism.

Philosophical positivism, the existentialist would maintain, treats the whole of reality including man as simply a system of data or things or objects which is fully amenable to the method of science. It seeks to explain man empirically as merely one thing or collection of things amongst other things. In other words it treats him as only a complicated aspect of the physical world. It ignores the truth that man is essentially a subject and not merely an object, that he is a first person event and not simply a third person event. It forgets that man is not merely a part of the world but also an originator of meaning and value in the world. In brief, it fails to appreciate that the world of objectivity can present itself as such only because man is not simply an object but also a subject. Thus even in their own exercise the meaning-giving explanations of science contradict the absolutist claims made on their behalf from the positivist standpoint. Hence, Merleau-Ponty remarks: 'Scientific points of view, according to which my existence is a moment of the world's, are always both naive and at the same time dishonest, because they take for granted, without explicitly mentioning it, the other point of view, namely that of consciousness, through which from the outset a world forms itself round me and begins to exist for me.'[1]

Existentialism also criticises idealism as an inadequate philosophical account of man. Idealism, it agrees, rightly emphasises that man in virtue of the power of subjectivity somehow constitutes the reality of the world as object. But it envisages this subjectivity as universal disembodied all-embracing spirit. The individual finite subject and the independent reality of material things are absorbed within the ambit of self-sufficient subjectivity and thought. Ultimately in idealism every reality, and man in particular, is rarefied to the status of a modification or manifestation of a comprehensive self or absolute spirit. The development of this tendency to ground the being of man in an enclosed and self-sufficient subjectivity can be traced through the philosophy of Descartes, Spinoza and Leibniz. It achieves its most complete expression in the philosophy of Hegel which envisages every aspect of reality as a moment in the progressive self-manifestation of an absolute, divine and utterly rational mind. According to existentialists this apparent exaltation of man in idealism is in fact a radical dehumanisation of him. It diminishes his authentic freedom, creativity and responsibility. It reduces his concrete, personal and embodied existence to merely a phase in the elaboration of an eternal inexorable logic.

Positivism emphasises that man is what he is only on a basis of materiality but underestimates the significance of his subjectivity. Idealism highlights the importance of man, as subjectivity but neglects the truth that this is not an absolute self-enclosed subjectivity but rather a subjectivity grafted through a body onto a physical world. Hence, the truth which existentialism accepts as the fundamental and irreducible starting point of authentic philosophical reflection is the description of man as an incarnate liberty. Its basic philosophical perspective is a view of man as that unique reality which is not just a thing in the world, nor a pure subjectivity, but precisely a free subjectivity which, as incarnate, opens out upon and is present to a world involving other people. Let us now consider how, as mentioned above, certain elucidations of this perspective have led to explicitly atheistic conclusions.

The development of existentialism along atheistic lines has been elaborated through reflection both upon man's free subjectivity and upon the incarnate situated character of this subjectivity. On the one hand it is proclaimed that the affirmation of God would undermine the exigencies of man's freedom and creativity. On the other hand it is maintained that the facticity of his incarnate situation precludes any affirmation of a divine source and purpose of human life. The ambiguity and paradox which characterise man as incarnate liberty constitute the ultimate, limiting and irreducible horizon of all meaning and value.

A profound solicitude to defend the reality and significance of human freedom is a constant feature of existentialist philosophy. It seeks to recall the individual from the inauthenticity of unthinking conformity with the *mores* of the group to a heightened awareness of his own possibility of radical choice and decision. In some cases, for example in the teaching of Kierkegaard, Marcel and Jaspers, the supreme expression of a truly appropriated human freedom is represented as a personalised openness, commitment and fidelity to God as the Freedom which makes other freedom possible. Thus, for instance, in Jaspers' estimation the deepest philosophical insight is the appreciation that man, the free *Existenz,* who as more than mere empirical being is the source of future possibilities, is such only as the gift of Transcendence.[2] More often, however, the existentialist defence of human freedom takes the form of rejecting all reference to God as incompatible with this freedom.

The philosophy of the will-to-power advanced by F. Nietzsche (1844–1900), who together with Kierkegaard figures as a founder of existentialism, is an impassioned eulogy of this form of atheism. He drew inspiration from Schopenhauer's (1788–1860) development of the Kantian 'thing-in-itself' into a theory that all phenomenal reality is a manifestation of an underlying restless will-to-live. In Nietzsche's philosophy of man this fundamental primacy of will becomes the unrestricted self-assertion of the exceptional individual who unequivocally proclaims the death of God and in doing so rejects the notion of any system of absolute and universal truth or value.[3] Belief in God and universal moral values is taken to be a sign of cowardice—an evasion of the challenge to be fully free. The individual, who transcends the mob and asserts his autonomous reality as will-to-power, chooses atheism as a necessary concomitant of the act whereby *he wills* that his own reality, as the superman (*der Uebermensch*) who transvalues all value, *shall be* the meaning of the earth.

This postulatory atheism of Nietzsche finds a close present-day parallel in the existentialist philosophy of Sartre. Sartre is the philosopher *par excellence* of human freedom. An unshakeable commitment to the absolute freedom of man and a ruthlessly honest acceptance of what he sees to be its implications is a characteristic feature of his entire philosophical endeavour.[4] Fundamental to this conception of man as absolute freedom is a denial of a universal human nature and *a fortiori* a denial of God as the intelligent creator of human nature.

In Sartre's estimation the only conception of human freedom worthy of the name is that which responsibly acknowledges itself as the absolute creative source and goal of the sense and value of life. The only value which is absolutely self-authenticating is the value of freedom itself. Man is truly man only in virtue of that continuous self-surpassing through which all his actions are given as their ultimate significance the quest of freedom itself as such.[5] Thus he openly espouses a humanism of total liberty which, as we noted in chapter one, he judges to be the true consequence of the exploration into subjectivity inaugurated by Descartes.

Sartre points out that although this view is certainly atheistic, and even although its elaboration can be seen as drawing out the full conclusions from a consistently atheistic position, nevertheless it does not gravitate around proofs for the non-existence of God. Rather, it maintains that even if God existed it would not make any difference from its point of view. Whether or not God exists, the only thing that counts is the acknowledgement of man as total freedom who in every circumstance wills only his own freedom. Consequently, even if man knew himself to be created, as a *free* created being he would resolutely stand over against God in radical independence.[6]

However, even though Sartre thus observes that in a certain sense an argued disproof of the existence of God is incidental to his rejection of Him, which is rooted rather in his passionate affirmation of human freedom as utterly autonomous, nevertheless he is fully convinced that the existence of God is in fact demonstrably incompatible with this conception of human freedom. He contrasts the free human condition with that of an artefact such as a book or a paper-knife. In the case of the latter it has been made by an artisan in accordance with his conception of it. It is made in a certain way to be of a particular kind and to serve a definite purpose. In brief, its essence precedes its existence and determines its existence. Sartre argues that it is a feature of theism that this priority of essence over existence is extended also to man. When we think of God as the creator we think of Him as a supernatural artisan. Just as the paper-

K

knife is manufactured by the artisan according to a pre-
conceived formula and definition so likewise each individual
man is a realisation of a certain conception which dwells in
the divine understanding.[7] The consequence of such a view
is that human existence, including human freedom, is
encompassed and determined by a divinely bestowed human
nature. The only way of truly being a man is through
conformity to God's conception of man. Thus the creativity
of human freedom is negated.

The atheistic existentialist, as described by Sartre, resists
this tendency to envisage the human condition in terms of a
human nature fashioned by a divine artisan. It proposes as
the true appraisal of man that he, unlike all artefacts, is the
being whose existence precedes its essence. Man first of all
exists and subsequently defines himself through his choices.
He is not initially definable because to begin with he is
nothing. Human existence is a spontaneous centre of
absolute freedom which decides for itself how it shall be.
There is no predetermined human nature or *a priori* system
of moral values to guide man's choices because there is no
God to predetermine such a nature or such values. If there
were a God, man's freedom would be an illusion. Since this
freedom is not an illusion, but rather the innermost reality
of man, we must abandon the affirmation of God and follow
the consequence of man's absolute freedom to its logical
conclusion. Nor is this a comforting conclusion in which the
same norms and values, which the out-of-date hypothesis of
God previously supported, are rediscovered in a new and
intrinsically assured conception of man's meaning and
destiny. 'The existentialist, on the contrary, finds it extremely
embarrassing that God does not exist, for there disappears
with Him all possibility of finding values in an intelligible
heaven. There can no longer be any good *a priori*, since there
is no infinite and perfect consciousness to think it. It is
nowhere written that "the good" exists, that one must be
honest or must not lie, since we are now upon the plane
where there are only men. . . . Everything is indeed per-

mitted if God does not exist.'[8] Man, in a godless world, is condemned to be free. He did not create himself but finds himself thrown into this world. His power is confined but his freedom is unrestricted. He has no guarantees but must choose, and in choosing decide, the sense and value of his life for which he alone is utterly responsible.

Thus Sartre's philosophy of man's absolute freedom as outlined in *Existentialism and Humanism*, and as elaborated more technically in *Being and Nothingness,* is radically critical not merely of theism but also of the various forms of 'optimistic atheism' which, as we have seen, are characteristic of nineteenth-century philosophy. These latter, no less than the former, are merely so many deceptions whereby men seek to hide from themselves the wholly voluntary nature of their existence. There is no independent order of meaning and value—whether this be conceived in terms of an absolute spirit, a communist society, or a rationalised technocracy—in which human freedom can be anchored as in an absolute norm of voluntary action. My freedom is not simply a matter of being capable of assenting to an independently meaningful order of being but of choosing what shall be the meaning of my life. Moreover, my choice, in whatever form of life it expresses itself, retains an irreducible quality of gratuitousness in that I cannot demonstrate the rectitude of my choice by any appeal to its conformity with norms or authorities beyond my freedom. There is no consideration which can affect my freedom decisively since it is this freedom itself which decides which considerations shall be effective. The man who convinces himself that he acts in accordance with a fixed objective moral requirement deceives himself and acts in bad faith. He is responsible for an alienation of himself which could have been avoided but which through his own cowardly self-indulgence was not.

This alienation through bad faith is avoided by men of good faith whose concrete actions have as their ultimate intended significance the quest of freedom itself as such. However, even those who are faithful to this aim of freedom can never, in Sartre's estimation, hope through any conceivable programme of concrete action to achieve complete human fulfilment. For the basic meaning of man's project as freedom is a desire to be God, a desire which is in principle unrealisable and, therefore, *a fortiori*, unrealised through any particular programme of action.[9]

This surprising view that man's fundamental project is an unrealisable desire to be God derives from certain general considerations of Sartre's ontology into which we shall not enter here.[10] They underpin a radical contrast which he affirms between, on the one hand, the inert, unthinking, undifferentiated, brute density of being-in-itself and, on the other hand, the being-for-itself of conscious freedom which is seen as a fissure in being-in-itself—a nothingness, a lack, a desire for the solidity of being-in-itself, an unsubstantial principle of meaning and project. The fundamental structure or truth of human freedom is to be a project of achieving a synthesis of being-in-itself-for-itself, of anchoring the nothingness, the desire, the lack which is being-for-itself in the fullness and density of being-in-itself. This identity of in-itself and for-itself, if achieved, would accomplish the reality of an *Ens causa sui*, a being which escapes brute contingency by being its own foundation. In a word, it would be God.

But such an ideal is in fact impossible and contradictory. The for-itself of conscious freedom obtains only in so far as it is a nothingness, a lack of being, a constant self-surpassing and, therefore, only inasmuch as it is in polar tension with the fullness and solidity of being-in-itself. Ever to achieve a state of identity with the in-itself, a state which might be said to obtain only at death, would be to cease being for-itself. Thus the fundamental project of man—the desire to be God—is a contradictory ideal incapable of realisation.[11] Only by acknowledging his absolute freedom is his existence authentic. But this freedom is ultimately of no avail. Beneath the remediable self-alienation of bad faith lies a deeper constitutional alienation of man as an unrealisable project. 'Thus the passion of man is the reverse of that of Christ, for man loses himself as man in order that God may be born. But the idea of God is contradictory and we lose ourselves in vain. Man is a useless passion.'[12].

Other existentialist writers, even if critical of Sartre's radical antithesis between the being-in-itself of things and the being-for-itself of conscious freedom, nevertheless endorse his contention that the existence of God is incompatible with an affirmation of the reality of human freedom. The philosophy of Merleau-Ponty is a good example of such qualified support. He insists that since our freedom always finds itself as a freedom involved in a concrete worldly situation it is inappropriate to speak of it as a total or absolute freedom.[13] His philosophy involves an illuminating account of this situated freedom in terms of a theory of the human body, understood not as a thing or object but as a pre-personal dimension of subjectivity through which man is constituted as present to a world. The body understood thus as 'body-subject' is a necessary if somewhat ambiguous mediator between the in-itself and the for-itself in the elaboration of human meaning and value.[14] However, although this philosophy is critical of the 'accursed lucidity' of Sartre's sharp oppositions it confirms his postulatory atheism inasmuch as it too precludes the affirmation of God as incompatible with even its own more restricted conception of human freedom.

In a certain sense it is imprecise to speak of Merleau-Ponty's philosophy as atheistic. Certainly he himself was reluctant to describe it in this way.[15] Such a description, he maintained, is essentially negative and involves a built-in reference to a theological viewpoint which introduces an extraneous bias into philosophical discussion. Seen from such a viewpoint all philosophy becomes a polemic between theism and anthropotheism—between an affirmation of God and a deification of man. In Merleau-Ponty's estimation philosophy today must question the underlying presumption of this approach, namely, that there is an absolute explanation of being in general and of man in particular so that the only point at issue is whether this explanation is to be sought in terms of the God of traditional theology or in terms of one of the modern versions of Promethean humanism. The genuinely philosophical approach is one whose reflections are not encapsulated within any general presumption that man will find in being any absolute meaning or assured destiny. Moreover, should it in fact turn out that no such meaning and destiny is to be found, the philosopher will not designate this conclusion as atheism. For to do so would be to revert to a no longer relevant theological appraisal of a philosophical position.

This reluctance of Merleau-Ponty to be located on either arm of the theist-atheist alternative is an illuminating illustration of the non-problematic absence of God which, as we noted at the end of chapter six, is a characteristic feature of much of contemporary culture and thought. It indicates how henceforth it may be increasingly difficult even to pose the problem of God since people tend less and less to relate to a divine reality as an ultimate point of reference from which to unfold, even by way of reaction, an account of the human condition.[16] Thus, although contemporary *a*-theism may have come historically to a reflective awareness of itself through an explicit reaction against a prevailing theistic view of reality, this built-in reference of atheism to theism is gradually disappearing. To a considerable extent atheism today tends less to be a result of a critique of religion or of proofs for God and tends more to be simply an incidental consequence of an unquestioningly accepted wholly secular way of envisaging and living out one's life.

When pressed, however, Merleau-Ponty readily agrees that although he personally might not use such terms in a presentation of his position, nevertheless it is in fact by traditional standards an undoubtedly atheistic position. In other words he admits that any affirmation of the existence of God is quite incompatible with his conception of the human condition. Moreover, he advances various arguments to show how and why this is so.

A concern to safeguard a certain conception of the contingency of man is the mainspring of Merleau-Ponty's refusal of theism.[17] By the 'contingency' of man he means more than the existential instability which, according to traditional metaphysics, characterises all material beings. He means, rather, man considered in his specific reality as a body-subject or situated freedom who is the mysterious source of worldly meaning and value. Man's contingency signifies that he is not completely determined by a system of necessary laws and causally linked events. On the contrary he is a weakness at the heart of nature who breaks the circuit of cosmic determinism and thereby renders possible the transformation of the anonymous realm of necessity into the autonomous world of history and culture.[18] Evaluated by the standard of physical necessity, the contingency which characterises man's liberty and temporal mode of being can indeed be called a weakness. But it would be pointless, in Merleau-Ponty's view, to consider it as a weakness which we should seek to explain in terms of something outside and beyond itself. It must be looked upon, not as something to be explained, but as the crowning glory of man which renders all meaning, explanation and value possible.

Thus, according to Merleau-Ponty, human contingency is a truly fundamental fact which resists all explanation because it is prior to any explanation as a condition of its possibility. Since it is precisely the mystery of human contingency which renders all explanation possible, to look for an explanation of human contingency itself would be a confusion of thought, a category mistake, which could only yield a distorted view of reality. Hence, his whole philosophy, which may be called a philosophy of contingency, is resolutely committed to defending human contingency against all the 'solutions' which would suppress it.

Because of this absolute commitment to the irreducibility of human contingency Merleau-Ponty repudiates a theistic interpretation of it. He argues that the theist affirms human contingency merely in order to derive from it the affirmation of a necessary being and thereby undermine the significance of this contingency which such an affirmation claims to explain. Theism merely utilises the power of philosophical wonderment, which should remain anchored in the miracle of human contingency, in order to eliminate both the wonderment and the contingency through recourse to divine transcendence. Such a divine explanation, no less than the various forms of naturalism and ideological humanism, destroys the ambiguity and creative spontaneity of man.[19] For if human contingency is explained in terms of the divine causality of a necessary being, everything reverts to the causal order, the order of strict determinism in which the future can be deduced from the past. But man as centre of indetermination, as source of meaning and value, as creator of history, is precisely the sort of reality whose future cannot be deduced from his past. He is not an inexorably linked set of events but rather an incarnate freedom who, in virtue of his contingency, creates the future. Hence, the affirmation of a necessary being must be rejected in defence of man's contingency.

This position has been criticised as depending upon too rigid a conception of causality.[20] It assumes that God could function as an explanation or exercise causality only in the same way as the strictly deterministic causality which controls the processes of nature. If this were so, man's liberty would indeed be compromised for such causality is incompatible with freedom in the effect. It is a causality in virtue of which the future unfolds inexorably and predictably from the present and the past. However, this is not the only legitimate sense in which causality may be envisaged. Even within our own experience we encounter situations which call for a more flexible conception of causality than that according to which the exercise of causality precludes the freedom of its effect. Consider, for example, the causality which accomplishes an expansion of subjectivity, which two persons undoubtedly exercise upon each other in a situation of authentic communication. Such causality does not destroy freedom but rather presupposes it and enriches it. Indeed, what effect could one person's discourse have upon another were the latter not freely disposed throughout to receive it attentively? It is argued that similar considerations, understood analogically, might be advanced in support of the contention that the creative causality of divine love is not incompatible with Merleau-Ponty's conception of human contingency. Further, it is argued that some such elucidation of human contingency is called for since this contingency or situated freedom of man is profoundly mysterious and puzzling. In seeking to safeguard it from solutions which would destroy it Merleau-Ponty treats it as a fundamental unquestionable fact. But to disengage the problem of contingency from unsatisfactory solutions is one matter, to ignore the problem itself is another. For it is not at all a self-explanatory fact about which no further questions can be asked. On the contrary it is a precarious, obscure and by no means fully intelligible reality. The question of its possible reference to a higher reality as its ultimate source is entirely pertinent.

However, in its whole orientation Merleau-Ponty's philosophy is insensitive to such a line of criticism. For it rejoices in the chiaroscuro of human contingency as the precarious source of meaning and value. Moreover, instead of seeking to resolve the complex ambiguity and paradox of this contingency by relating it to a higher source, its tendency is rather to reinforce these characteristics by relating human contingency, downwards as it were, to the profound obscurity of our pre-personal bodily subjectivity. As described by him, our ambiguous condition of situated freedom which renders possible our conscious elaboration of meaning and value is preceded by, and emerges without any radical discontinuity from, the meaning-giving character of our basic reality as a pre-conscious body-subject.

This conception of man as a body-subject is the touchstone

of Merleau-Ponty's philosophy. In contrast with the Cartesian conception of the body as merely an extended thing, he maintains that the human body itself, as such, is the fundamental form of subjectivity, the animating centre of various fields of meaning. It is in and of the world but is situated there as the meaning-giving principle around which and in virtue of which the world assembles itself as a meaningful environment. In a crucial manner the historical circumstance and concrete organisation of one's body is the fundamental wellspring of the meanings and goals which one's world presents. The body is essentially a world-builder or intentionality. For example, in a not yet free or conscious manner it opens up the various dimensions of one's existence as bound to the world, such as the dimensions of oriented space in virtue of which one's journeys are pleasant or arduous, or the dimensions of sexual meaning which resonate throughout one's being at the onset of puberty. The body as body-subject institutes a primitive pre-conceptual dialogue with the world—a pre-conscious structuration of the world. It knows more of the world than I consciously do myself. It originates a self-surpassing wellspring of meaning and affective tonality which is never totally conceptualised.[21] Moreover, all our free and conscious promotion of meaning, including all philosophical reflection, is basically an appropriation and transformation of this deep mysterious presence of our body to a world. 'All that we are, we are on the basis of a *de facto* situation which we appropriate to ourselves and which we ceaselessly transform by a sort of *escape* which is never an unconditioned freedom.'[22]

Thus the ambiguous situated freedom or contingency that characterises human existence as a conscious source of meaning and value is in reality simply a higher level expression of the self-surpassing meaning-giving existence of the pre-personal body-subject. Hence, to attempt to situate, as theism proposes to do, the ultimate source of all meaning and value in a divine mind is to undermine one of man's most significant, mysterious and distinctive properties, namely, that in and through the mediation of his body he is a world-builder, an origin of the miracle of meaning. The realm of consciously adopted meaning and purpose can be intelligibly discussed only within the context of the conditions through which it can emerge, namely, our temporal presence to a world instituted by our body. Therefore Merleau-Ponty confidently concludes that 'if we rediscover time beneath the subject, and if we relate to the paradox of time those of the body, the world, the thing, and other people, we shall understand that beyond these there is nothing to understand.'[23]

This philosophy of the body-subject as the precarious but irreducible source of all meaning and value involves a repudiation of any epistemological or ontological absolute and *a fortiori* of any divine absolute.[24] Each body-subject through its intersubjective involvement with other body-subjects advances the cultural legacy of meaning which has already been historically articulated by previous generations. This cultural sediment of acquired meaningful language, this 'flesh of history' which constitutes our situation and which we as body-subjects in turn transform and advance, gives us the illusion of access to a realm of absolute truths.[25] It is a repository of numerous already enunciated truths which have become the automatically accepted common property of men. But this already spoken language in which these firmly accepted truths have found expression and realisation is itself a bodily historical fact. It lies rooted in the darkness and contingency of the world-building activity of the pre-personal body-subject.[26]

The final outcome of this conception of Merleau-Ponty's is a metaphysical viewpoint according to which reality is intelligible not in principle but simply in fact. It is so in virtue of its accessibility to man as a meaning-giving body-subject who illuminates the density and darkness of being in which he finds himself involved. This meaning-giving reality of our human existence as body-subject is itself a situated, contingent, factual existence. Man as the source of worldly meaning does not radically transcend the facticity of the world. Rather he fully participates in it as a factual moment of light which illuminates the surrounding darkness. Meaning and value are not denied of being but the absolute meaning and value traditionally attributed to it by metaphysics is rejected. Genuine metaphysical consciousness is seen to consist in an enduring wonder at the ultimate fact of the body-subject as a contingent source of the factual and contingent intelligibility of being.[27]

Obviously this metaphysical viewpoint precludes the affirmation of a divine absolute. In particular, Merleau-Ponty points out, it precludes the Christian belief in God the Father as the creator of heaven and earth.[28] Such a belief, he argues, undermines the conception of man as an irreducible source of genuine historical meaning and value and engenders a stoical attitude of unavailing quietism. For it envisages God as an absolute being in whom all knowledge, beauty and goodness have been achieved from all eternity. Human endeavour is rendered meaningless and the *status quo* invested with the stamp of divine approval. No endeavour on our part can add to the perfection of reality since this is already fully realised in an infinite manner. There is literally nothing to do or to accomplish. We are petrified and impotent beneath a divine gaze, reduced to the condition of *visible things*. All our inner resources are alienated by an infinite wisdom which has already disposed all things well.

Moreover, Merleau-Ponty argues, through belief in the God of Christianity we are alienated in our relationship both with the world and with other people. The Church becomes our centre of gravity rather than the world with a consequent relativisation of all simply secular endeavour. Likewise, in our relationships with other people we become intolerant and exclusive. The specifically human project of inter-subjective participation in the constitution of a precarious and never absolutely guaranteed world of meaning and value is negated. Such a conception, which envisages truth and value as the tentative achievement of a contingent human community, is rejected in the name of a system of divinely guaranteed truths. The believer situates the origin of meaning and value above the level of human endeavour and dialogue. He claims a privileged access to absolute truth and his beliefs are accorded a sacred value in virtue of which he can piously commit his enemies to the flames.[29]

Thus in rejecting belief in a divine absolute, Merleau-Ponty is motivated not simply by metaphysical but also by moral considerations. He is concerned to safeguard the mutual recognition of man by man as well as to defend the genuine metaphysical consciousness which affirms as a fundamental fact the meaning-giving virtuosity of the contingent body-subject. The metaphysical and moral consciousness, he assures us, perishes at the touch of the absolute.[30]

Throughout the literature of atheistic existentialism considerable weight is attached to such moral considerations. Inasmuch as the world embodies manifest dimensions of misery and innocent suffering, the affirmation of God is said to be morally intolerable and inasmuch as man as an incarnate freedom is the autonomous source of meaning and value throughout the world, the affirmation is said to be morally unnecessary. It is seen as bad faith to advance speculative explanations and justifications of an absurd and unjustifiable world. The authentic human reaction to evil is not one which seeks to explain it away but rather one which combats it and rebels against it.

The writings of Camus typify this existentialist attitude of heroic atheism. In his novels and essays Camus advocates a defiant rejection of God in the name of a loving solidarity with mankind in its ignoble condition of suffering and eventual death. Dismayed by man's abandoned condition, the rebel advances from an initial attitude of blasphemy, through an outright denial of God and of all alternative secular absolutes, to a freely bestowed outpouring of loving solicitude for his humiliated fellow man.[31] Existential philanthropy is chosen instead of moral theology which is seen as logically fostering indifference to the human predicament. For example, Rieux the atheist doctor in *The Plague* remarks that if he believed in an all-powerful God he 'would cease curing the sick and leave that to Him'.[32] He is an atheist because he believes that authentic morality consists in 'fighting against creation as he found it'.[33]

Similar considerations are advanced by F. Jeanson, a close associate and philosophical disciple of Sartre. In a study in which he seeks to elaborate the 'faith' of an unbeliever he repudiates religious belief in an infinite being in favour of an enthusiastic commitment to the resourcefulness of human freedom in the promotion of a loving solidarity amongst men.[34] Religious belief he takes to be a function of fear. It arises when man, in view of his insecurity and vulnerability, chooses to believe in an omnipotent God and to confess the radical impotence of man. Instead of such an inhuman abdication of responsibility Jeanson proposes that notwithstanding man's perilous condition and utter lack of ultimate guarantees he should take the risk of having faith in a collective human project of truth and justice. He concedes that man experiences himself as a brute fact rooted in a condition of basic ontological contingency. He argues, however, that any man having chosen to accept his existence, having chosen to live and thereby entered upon the way of human meaning, should stake his trust in the co-operative capacity of mankind to invest life with meaning and value. Man must push beyond the various illusory beliefs in an already assured salvation to a courageous faith in his own efforts which has no other foundation than this faith itself and the endeavours which it engenders. His final conclusion is that if one were required to adopt a creed one should believe only in that which one wagers to achieve through human resources alone.[35]

Having noted various characteristic features of atheistic existentialism we are now in a position to indicate certain general conclusions concerning its importance in formulating an overall appraisal of the development of contemporary atheism. Moreover, as we mentioned at the beginning of this chapter, we hope in the light of these conclusions to reach a point of departure for a contemporary re-examination of the problem of God. In effect, we will indicate how certain features of the contemporary situation in the evolution of philosophical atheism suggest the appropriateness and even the urgent necessity of considering anew the possibility of a valid affirmation of God. Such a reconsideration will be undertaken in chapter eight.

In various ways existentialism reveals itself as a mature and self-conscious statement of a thoroughgoing humanism of liberty which has been seeking ever more adequate expression since Descartes' revolutionising affirmation of the philosophical primacy of human subjectivity. It does so, for example, in the supreme importance which it attaches, most notably in the case of Sartre, to man's creative freedom. It does so, also, in its contention, stressed by Merleau-Ponty, that the effective exercise of such freedom is confined within a this-worldly context of exclusively human meaning and purpose. It does so, finally, in the way in which its proponents, such as Camus and Jeanson, insist that the only authentic moral stance is one of reliance upon human resources alone and a refusal of any recourse to a divine explanation of the human condition as morally reprehensible.

The existentialists' decision to exclude on moral grounds any divine explanation of man has as its theoretical counterpart an exclusively phenomenological account of the world of human experience. Admittedly, there is general agreement that 'the transphenomenal being of what exists *for consciousness* is itself in itself', i.e. that being exists not merely in so far as it appears, but also in itself.[36] It is, however, equally insistently maintained that this transphenomenal being is in itself quite meaningless. Human subjectivity is taken to be the exclusive source and norm of the meaning and value of being.[37] Hence philosophical investigation which unfolds as a descriptive elucidation of the foundations of the world of human experience seeks these foundations within the resources of human subjectivity itself. It seeks the foundations of experience in those pervasive characteristics of experience, such as freedom, embodiment, temporality and inter-subjectivity, which render it intrinsically possible. This account of the world of experience in terms of the basic properties of subjectivity encountered within human experience itself is taken as the exclusive source of the meaning and value of being. Any appeal to a trans-human principle of ontological intelligibility—for example, a divine mind—is strictly excluded. Irrespective of any anomalies and paradoxes which it may involve, the principle that man is the measure of being is accepted as an ultimate and irreducible fact.[38]

It can scarcely be denied that this position does give rise to serious anomalies and paradoxes. Indeed the very project of philosophy as a response to a specifically human need for dependable light and truth about being in general and human existence in particular appears, on this view, to be ultimately unavailing. The elucidation of meaning and value is brought to an abrupt halt in a cul-de-sac of sheer contingency and facticity. Moreover, the road to any further enquiry, which might resolve the seemingly meaningless character of being in itself and the seemingly brute fact of man as a situated freedom and contingent source of meaning, is methodologically sealed. The repercussions of this acceptance of ultimate meaninglessness manifest themselves in a variety of explicit philosophical tensions. One might cite, for example, the tension between the impersonal meaning disclosed by scientific explanation and the human meaning disclosed by phenomenological description; or the tension in Merleau-Ponty's description of personal free subjectivity, as at once quite original in character and yet in perfect continuity with anonymous pre-personal bodily subjectivity; or, again, the manifold tensions inherent in Sartre's view of man as a contradictory project, a futile passion. Perhaps the most serious objection with which existentialism finds itself confronted is that although in its phenomenological descriptions of the knowing subject's presence to a world it consciously avoids the inadequacies of both empiricism and idealism, nevertheless in its ontological interpretation of this knowledge it lapses into a philosophical dualism involving versions of precisely these views which it has criticised. In other words, in taking contingent human subjectivity as the exclusive measure of the meaning and value of being is it not inevitably committed, in the final analysis, to an ontology of brute fact and an idealism of signification?[39]

Nevertheless, notwithstanding these and other difficulties involved in its narrowly phenomenological approach, atheistic existentialism is not disposed to qualify its contention that man is the exclusive measure of the meaning and value of being. Thus, unlike its theistic counterpart, it is not prepared to relativise its conception of man as source of meaning and value by understanding it in a wider context of assent and fidelity to an encompassing mystery of intrinsically intelligible being. One may surmise that this disinclination of atheistic existentialism to pursue any such approach, which favours an affirmation of a divine source of the intelligibility of being, is motivated not simply by theoretical and methodological considerations but also by its conviction that any affirmation of God is morally reprehensible. In other words, the axiological or moral judgement that an affirmation of God is incompatible with the requirements of human freedom reinforces the methodological considerations which make man the measure of being, and functions as a moral deterrent against any relativisation of this viewpoint. The outcome is, as Sartre observes, a decision to adhere heroically to the full conclusions of a consistently atheistic humanism no matter how disconcerting or paradoxical these may be, rather than have recourse to a morally indefensible affirmation of God.

However, although atheistic existentialism emphasises both the 'anthropocentrism' and the passionate affirmation

L

of freedom which characterise the post-Cartesian humanism of liberty, it is uniquely reserved in its appraisal of this humanism's possibilities. Its view of man's condition and his prospects differs decisively from the confident expectations of the various forms of nineteenth-century atheistic human-ism. In taking seriously the full conclusions of an atheistic position it refuses to substitute any deification of man for the belief in the traditional God which it has rejected. It sees no absolute guarantees or assured salvation of man in any theory of the inevitable triumph of brotherly love, or in the advent of a communist society, or in the possibilities of technological rationalisation. As Sartre sees it: 'Everything is indeed permitted if God does not exist, and man is in consequence forlorn, for he cannot find anything to depend upon either within or outside himself.'[40] This does not mean that according to atheistic existentialism one should be unconcerned about the promotion of a human order of truth and justice. It does mean, however, that the promotion of such an order is wholly dependent upon the decisions and actions issuing forth from man's precarious freedom and that its eventual achievement is in no way assured. We must resolutely accept the basic fact about man that he is an utterly inexplicable moment of light in the darkness and opaqueness of being, a mysterious principle of freedom, love, meaning and justice; grafted, through his body, to a world of hazard, absurdity, contingency and ambiguity. The human project which we cherish as an epiphany of meaning and value may, either individually or collectively, fail upon the way like an unfinished sentence.

The predominant ethos of existentialist thought is sensitively conveyed by Camus in the following striking passage towards the end of his book *The Rebel*:

The words which reverberate for us at the confines of this long adventure of rebellion, are not formulae for optimism, for which we have no possible use in the extremities of our unhappiness, but words of courage and intelligence which, on the shores of the eternal seas, even have the qualities of virtue.

No possible form of wisdom today can claim to give more. Rebellion indefatigably confronts evil, from which it can only derive a new impetus. Man can master, in himself, everything that should be mastered. He should rectify in creation everything that can be rectified. And after he has done so, children will still die unjustly even in a perfect society. Even by his greatest effort, man can only propose to diminish, arithmetically, the sufferings of the world. But the injustice and the suffering of the world will remain and, no matter how limited they are, they will not cease to be an outrage. Dmitri Karamazov's cry of 'Why?' will continue to resound through history . . .

We offer as an example, the only original rule of life today: to learn to live and to die, and in order to be a man, to refuse to be a god.[41]

It is on this somewhat sombre note that our review of the historical development of contemporary atheism comes to a close. In the course of our consideration we have witnessed a significant evolution in the relationship between the philosophical notions of alienation and atheism. We have seen how the traditional conviction that man would be alienated unless he interpreted his personal and collective existence in terms of a divine creator has, since the emergence of modern science and Cartesian philosophy, progressively given way to the view that man is alienated precisely in so far as he interprets his existence in terms of a divine creator. We have seen the development of this new viewpoint in Kant's vindication of the autonomy of science and morality and his critique of revealed religion; in Hegel's rejection of the traditional understanding of divine transcendence; in Feuerbach's atheistic anthropology; and in the Marxist and Positivist rejection of God in favour of an exclusively secular humanism. In these various positions we have seen how the appraisal that belief in God is a source of alienation has been accompanied by an alternative and even optimistic evaluation of human destiny. Finally, however, in atheistic existentialism we have seen how the rejection of God in defence of the transcendence, creativity and liberty of man has been accompanied by a frank admission of the obscure, unvindicated and ultimately uncertain outcome of this creative autonomy of man.

In certain respects it appears as though we have al most come full circle. Both the godless man as envisaged by traditional belief and the contemporary atheist as self-portrayed in existentialism are thrown back upon their own resources and can find neither in the world nor in history any absolute or ultimate vindication of the human project. Needless to say there are significant differences in the two conceptions. For example, the unbeliever today enjoys a more effective control over his life and project than did his other-self, the unbeliever of former times. He is also more aware of all that his subjectivity and freedom implies, and his denial of God should not be interpreted as a wilful repudiation of his responsibility for promoting a world of meaning and value. Nevertheless, common to both conceptions of the unbeliever is a sharp awareness of his inescapably forlorn and perilous condition. He is clearly seen to be without any dependable basis for confidence that his project of meaning and value will prevail within its encompassing milieu of sheer contingency and ultimate unintelligibility.

In this context the following question presents itself. Does not contemporary atheism, which re-states in a more refined and reflective fashion the traditional correlation of godlessness and ultimate unintelligibility, challenge the spirit of enquiry to explore the possibility of a new vindication of ultimate intelligibility in terms of a more refined and reflective affirmation of God? Such an affirmation, to be genuinely successful, would have to overcome not only the theoretical objections to the coexistence of man and God but also the axiological rejection of any affirmation of God as morally reprehensible and an alienation of human freedom and subjectivity. The difficulty of such an undertaking has undoubtedly been increased by the objections which have emerged in various stages of the evolution of contemporary atheism. However, to some extent this evolution itself confirms the appropriateness of such an undertaking. For it has shown in its progression through various unavailing secular absolutes that the denial of God is not a matter of little consequence which leaves our confidence in the bright world of meaning and value at least as well founded and assured as it was before the denial. On the contrary it shows that such a denial strikes at the very roots of any presumption of an ultimate and abiding intelligibility. Hence, for anyone in whom the desire and hope for such intelligibility is not yet fully extinguished it constitutes an appeal to reconsider the possibility of a theoretically and morally acceptable affirmation of God. In response to this appeal we propose in our final chapter to outline one possible approach to such an affirmation.

8

Chiaroscuro of Hope

In the concluding remarks of chapter seven we related the problem of God to the context of human hope. We intimated that to maintain hope in ultimate and abiding intelligibility is in the final analysis equivalent to maintaining hope in the affirmation of God. More concretely it is to persist in a joyful expectation that notwithstanding its intrinsically precarious condition the human project of meaning and value is a dependable enterprise assured of a happy outcome because it is founded and guaranteed by an intelligent personal creator. That this hope in an assured human destiny could be sustained only by such a divine principle is, paradoxically, one of the conclusions of the evolution of contemporary atheism, which has progressively undermined man's original uncritical hope or confidence that his complete fulfilment is absolutely assured if not by divine then at least by human means. What atheism requires of a man today is that he consciously live out a fully and exclusively human life without any ultimate hope. What theism must argue in support of its affirmation of God is that by abandoning such hope one is excluding a fundamental dimension of a fully human life, i.e. diminishing the possibilities of human creativity available to man.

By thus relating the problem of God to the context of human hope we are enabled to draw out certain considerations which should not be overlooked in a discussion of the problem. For example, we are adverted to the decidedly personal character of an affirmation of God, particularly in the present age. This does not mean that an affirmation of God is without rational justification—a blind leap in the dark or even a reversion to an infantile form of wish-fulfilment. It does mean, however, that more than purely speculative considerations must be taken into account in an adequate discussion of such an affirmation.

The affirmation of God does not fall within the sphere of objective knowledge which is the usual operation of human understanding. Such knowledge is characteristically concerned with physical objects which stand over against us in experience and which can be more and more effectively comprehended in a detached impersonal manner by ongoing scientific research. God is not a component or object within this field of empirical investigation. Rather He is envisaged, in part at least, as its supra-objective intelligent source who can be known only supra-objectively or metaphysically. A certain personal willingness to undertake the sort of enquiry involved in the attainment of such metaphysical knowledge is called for on the part of the knowing subject who finds himself naturally more at home, and assured of greater unanimity, at the strictly scientific level of empirically verifiable thought. For he lives today in a culture pervasively animated by a positivistic presumption of the unimportance and futility of any metaphysical quest for an ultimate intelligible foundation of the merely factual intelligibility of empirical being. In view of the materially and culturally enriching practical consequences of the purely scientific habit of mind, he is tempted to accept unquestioningly the philosophical absolutisation of scientific method and to ignore as unproductive the specifically human capacity to raise and pursue the question of the ultimate meaning and value of being in general and of human existence in particular. Attention to this question and to the metaphysical mode of reflection appropriate to its elucidation involves a freely exercised decision to remain open and responsive to the rational requirements of every level of human enquiry and not merely to those amenable to a limited but particularly influential methodology.

The personal involvement of one's free subjectivity in any projected affirmation of God is further illustrated by the fact that such an affirmation has a direct and profound bearing upon one's appraisal of oneself. It is not the sort of affirmation that can be received with the same detached equanimity that one accepts scientific information about physical objects. Rather its acceptance involves a willingness to see oneself in a completely new light as fundamentally dependent. In the believing culture of earlier times one was animated by a lively hope that through one's philosophical reflection one might come to see oneself in this light. For such dependence was envisaged as wholly good for man —a saving dependence upon the truly dependable. However, we have seen how the development of contemporary atheism, nourished by the modern ideal of human freedom and autonomy, has construed the conception of dependence upon God as a threat to the claims of human subjectivity and thus as a source of human alienation. Hence the affirmation of God as an ultimate principle of dependable intelligibility no longer appears as a human goal to be pursued or hoped for. On the contrary such an affirmation appears as unavailable to any man of authentic subjectivity, even as odious and to be positively avoided. The metaphysical desire for a principle of ultimate intelligibility is confronted with the objection that the affirmation of such a principle would be destructive of human subjectivity. Thus fidelity to what are taken to be the exigencies of subjectivity engenders a complete despair of any affirmation of a principle of ultimate intelligibility. Further, this despair itself promotes indifference to any metaphysical sense of wonder or line of reflection which tends in the direction of such an affirmation. Instead, the attitude that is cultivated and reinforced is one which seeks an exclusively human interpretation of any mysterious aspects of experience which nourish such metaphysical inquiry.

Perhaps, therefore, it is not so surprising that on an increasing scale traditional metaphysical discussion of the existence and nature of God fails to command much respect or even attention. The claims of the various metaphysical proofs for God are commonly ignored or briefly dismissed as unworthy of serious consideration. Even people who acknowledge the plausibility of their argumentation fail in many cases to achieve a self-involving assent to their conclusion. Three centuries of modern philosophy and the atheism which it has engendered cast an inescapable shadow between the notional comprehension of the verbal meaning of these proofs and a concrete existential comprehension of them as genuine disclosures of reality. It is as though in the wake of modern thought the world which we apprehend, and concomitantly our mode of apprehending it, have so changed that a new reality may be said to have superseded that of which the traditional proofs for God speak. Moreover, as we have already remarked, the language of human subjectivity through which this new reality is comprehended appears to exclude that hope or expectation of attaining an affirmation of God which animated the traditional attempts to argue to such an affirmation.

Hence the root of the philosophical problem of God today lies at a deeper level than a consideration of how one might show that, irrespective of the challenge of modern atheism, a valid metaphysical proof for His existence can still be formulated. It is rather, in the first place, a problem of considering how one might rationally evoke the hope in an affirmation of God which seems essential to the self-involving character of any argument in favour of this affirmation. In other words the problem is to show that, notwithstanding the contrary declarations made in the name of the exigencies of human subjectivity, the affirmation of God can be envisaged as an attainable goal expressing man's greatest and most enriching achievement.

Because of this requirement of activating hope in God in an age which is largely without such hope, the task of ration-

ally justifying an affirmation of His existence is undoubtedly
more difficult today than in the ages of belief when such
hope was already pre-reflectively operative in virtue of a
culturally pervasive religious faith. In exploring the possibility of a renewal of this hope it should be borne in mind
that hope relates more directly to the theme of man's
destiny than to that of his origins. Thus hope in God refers
more directly to the conception of Him as the supremely
desirable good who assures the fulfilment of man's project
than to the conception of Him as the creative first cause of
all finite being including man. Ultimately, of course, hope
in God involves as a justifying condition the affirmation of
Him as provident creator. But the hope itself bears directly
upon the conception of God as man's supreme good. Moreover, it is this conception which is more directly disputed
by contemporary atheism than the conception of God as
the creative first cause of which the traditional proofs speak.
Indeed the absence of hope in God conceived as man's
supreme good is a major contributory factor in the contemporary indifference to the viewpoint of these proofs. For
since such hope is seen as unavailing, the proofs are presumed
to be humanly irrelevant illusions.

In view of this situation it would seem that an approach
to vindicating an affirmation of God today, if it is to be
really apposite, should centre upon this alleged incom-
patibility between the exigencies of subjectivity and hope
in God. Rather than merely dwelling upon criticism of
particular assertions, this approach should seek to give a
positive account of these exigencies. It should seek to show
that they can be illuminatingly envisaged in a way which
discloses how hope in God need not appear as ultimately
incompatible but rather as truly consonant with them.
Ideally such an approach should adduce this compatibility
of hope in God with the claims of subjectivity in a manner
which could be shown to imply an actual affirmation of His
existence.

In the remaining pages of this study we will consider

briefly how such an approach might be developed. The preliminary nature of these remarks must be emphasised. They are by no means envisaged as an adequately developed philosophical justification of an affirmation of God. Such a project would be an immensely complex and difficult undertaking which should and will be taken up in a separate study. Hence to avoid conveying a misleading impression it is important to stress that the considerations indicated in this chapter are not intended to be taken as providing a decisive refutation of the serious case which, as we have seen, can be made for philosophical atheism. They are rather an anticipatory outline of the kind of assertions which would have to be painstakingly established in a metaphysically justified affirmation of God today. They intimate how such an affirmation might be intelligibly proposed in the circumstances of the contemporary preoccupation with the exigencies of human subjectivity. An adequate critical confirmation of this proposal and its presuppositions would involve such extensive and searching argumentation and such detailed attention to genuine difficulties that it is, as has been said, more properly a subject for further study in its own right.

When we speak of the claims of human subjectivity we refer chiefly to those distinctively self-assertive qualities of man in virtue of which he transcends the sheer factuality of thing-like existence and freely constitutes himself and his world. Man makes himself human by spontaneously transforming his given field of experience, including his experience of his own states and activities, into a world of meaning and value. The creativity or freedom of this human project of meaning and value is both contextually dependent and expansive. Moreover, it is precisely through the actual expansion of this situated freedom that the self-constitution of subjectivity is accomplished.

Inasmuch as we accept the life with which we find ourselves naturally endowed we may be said to choose our reality as a situated subject of immediate lived experience. We do not, however, freely determine how such experience shall appear. As Merleau-Ponty remarks, underlying free subjectivity there is a deeper bodily subjectivity through which the field of immediate human experience assembles itself. The field of immediate experience as such is not the true *métier* of our freedom.

The effective exercise of this freedom is more apparent in the persevering dedication and inventive ingenuity through which we strive to elaborate the field of experience into a universe of scientific meaning and truth. This exercise of freedom in the quest of objective truth is undoubtedly an enriching and liberating activity. Nevertheless, its goal and inspiration is not directly the constitution of free subjectivity or the realisation of how one would have things be, but rather the achievement of a detached impersonal view of how things are.

The explicit self-assertion of free subjectivity expresses itself more directly in the practical endeavour through which it progressively transmutes the world of intelligently comprehended experience into a cultural world of humanly intended meaning and value. Here the expansive reality of free subjectivity proclaims itself not only as a genuine characteristic of actual being but also as a criterion of desirable being. From this perspective of human freedom the axiological possibility of being appears to extend beyond its ontological actuality. One can appreciate the force of Heidegger's beautiful image of man as the shepherd of being or Jaspers' conception of free *Existenz* as the source of what might be and should be but is not yet and perhaps shall not be.

In this context of the origination and realisation of freely adopted cultural ideals one can deepen and clarify a conception of the person as an absolute value.[1] Being a free and intelligent subject of creative possibilities he is a reality of intrinsically worthwhile and never merely instrumental significance. As Kant observed he must always be considered as an end in himself and never simply as a means. Further, his creativity extends beyond the promotion of various particular goods, such as physical well-being, social order, scientific comprehension and aesthetic achievement, to an actualisation of unconditionally self-authenticating moral values. These are values which are directly involved in an ideal of the fullest possible realisation of every person as a free intelligent subjectivity. They are constitutive of the expansive liberation of the possibilities of personal being as such. The sort of values involved in this ideal are those of truth, freedom, justice and love. The ideal itself might be outlined as the accomplishment of the mutual loving recognition of liberated persons in a kingdom of truth and justice.

Thus man encounters his personhood as at once a subject and a goal of absolute value. He recognises that a requirement of himself as a person is the actualisation of those unconditional personal values, such as truth, freedom, justice and love, through which his irreplaceable reality as a free subjectivity expansively achieves itself. Moreover, he realises that this moral order through which the goal of personal liberation is advanced is utterly dependent upon him for its constitution. A human order of moral values could not be established by divine decree because it involves as an essential feature the exercise of human consent. A moral order can be advanced towards realisation only by being intelligently conceived and freely willed by man.

In this unnecessitated activity of freely willing the actualisation of an order of unconditional moral values, the human subject may truly be said to constitute himself and his world. Transcending the context of how things factually are, he projects an ideal of an intrinsically worthwhile state of affairs and freely commits himself to the implementation of this ideal. It is not necessary to involve any reference to God in a description of this advancement of a moral order. Its intrinsic possibility and coherence are adequately portrayed in purely secular terms concerning the creativity, freedom and transcendence proper to man. Considered from this axiological point of view, man as an irreducible well-spring of self-authenticating moral values can indeed be called an absolute.

It is noteworthy, however, that although this humanly intended moral order is promoted as an absolute in the order of value it does not present itself as an intrinsically assured goal. It represents an unconditionally worthwhile ideal but its actual achievement is by no means guaranteed. It is not ontologically self-vindicating notwithstanding its axiologically absolute and self-authenticating character.

If we judge man's incarnate historical mode of being to be the only ontological foundation for a projected order of meaning and value then our confidence in such an order can be no stronger than our confidence in the human mode of being itself. However, when we reflect upon the human mode of being we realise that although it is intrinsically worthwhile as a free and intelligent source of creative possibilities it is so in an inherently contingent, situated and precarious manner. Hence the human project of achieving a real order which will be completely and reliably characterised by personal and moral attributes can appear in a tragic perspective as unattainable because of the constitutionally frail, contingent and finite character of its human source.

In so far as man's contingent reality is taken as an ultimate unintelligible fact it calls in question the abiding significance and reliability of any project of meaning and value which he promotes. For however inherently admirable a particular human ordering of affairs may appear it does not present itself as being a more fundamental expression of reality than the inescapable fact of man's existential instability and vulnerability. The truth, freedom, justice and love which he brings to light throughout being are always a limited truth, a conditioned freedom, an imperfect justice and a precarious love. They appear within an encompassing context of ontological contingency, finitude and evil which is sharply illustrated by the inevitable death of each individual and the possible extinction of the entire human community. Seen from this perspective, fortuitousness, contingency and sheer facticity appear to be basic and insurmountable dimensions of reality, more fundamental in the last analysis than the tenuous pattern of personal and moral character-istics into which we seek to assemble all the resources of being. A heroic moral gesture, enacted in full awareness and acceptance of its ultimate insignificance and futility, would seem to be the most that man might reasonably expect or require of himself.

However, in the practical witness of life we find that we repudiate the ontologically precarious and accidental status ascribed by this view to the realm of personal and moral values. Through a remarkable expression of freedom we can determine ourselves to live these values not simply as self-authenticating but also as self-vindicating. We can live them as though they were *really* and not simply *axiologically* absolute, unconditional and trans-circumstantial. We *exercise* them as a more authentic epiphany of the ground of reality than sheer contingency, facticity and finitude. We are repeatedly reminded by concrete example that men consider it a more authentic witness to the mystery of reality to die for freedom, truth, justice and love than to live in acquiescence to the ultimacy of the limitations which encom-pass them as humanly experienced. We must reckon with this free affirmation, embodied in lived performance, that to fall victim to the power of contingency in defence of such values is not, despite appearances, a diminution of their reality but on the contrary an expansive disclosure that they have a more fundamental reality than have facticity, contingency and death.

This free existential affirmation of the ultimately personal and moral character of reality is not an arbitrary option. In various ways, and differently for different people, it is at least rationally prompted if not strictly necessitated. It may be prompted, for example, by fidelity to our spirit of enquiry which as a drive for comprehensive understanding of all reality envisages this reality as in principle not absurd but, rather, truly intelligible. Or again it may be prompted by any of a range of 'depth-experiences' such as experiences of intersubjectivity, of moral obligation, of beautiful or awe-inspiring phenomena.[2] For instance, a profound sense of the absolute demands of a self-authenticating moral ideal may inspire an existential commitment to the fundamentally personal character of reality on the grounds that a coherent proclamation of a compelling moral ideal presupposes its ontological realisability.

A comprehensive treatment of the problem of God would involve a detailed appraisal of these rational springs of our free existential affirmation of the fundamentally personal and moral quality of reality. Here, however, we are more directly concerned with drawing attention to the striking fact of this existentially exercised affirmation. In effect we find that we can and do freely involve ourselves in the encompassing world of our experience as though it really were in principle meaningful and good and not simply as though it merely should be so. In our existential response to the solicitations of experience we live out an outraged denial of the seemingly accidental and ontologically undependable character of the personal dimensions of reality. For example, in the activity of loving another person we exercise a commitment to the non-accidental character of the personal dimensions of their reality. In the expression of such love we refuse to accept as ontologically ultimate and decisive the loved one's contingency and facticity. We resist any such suggestion as incongruous with the creative response to his lovableness which we find is required of us, a creative response of which we find ourselves capable in the expression of our love. For we find that through a self-involving expression of our subjectivity we can, at least symbolically, overcome the seeming ultimacy of meaninglessness and contingency and enact in the exercise of our lives an affirmation of the ultimately personal character of being. We can freely determine ourselves to respond confidently to our experience of the world and other people as though the reign of meaning and value not merely should be the case but somehow really is so in principle and can be hoped to be effectively and reliably actualised. We find that such a response, which accords with the self-affirming *élan* of human subjectivity, inspires a more creative and enriching exercise of personhood than does resigned acceptance of ultimate absurdity.

Through this inventive exercise of our freedom we postulate the attainability of, and commit ourselves to making good, a fundamentally personal and moral order of reality. We can be said to choose, albeit not arbitrarily, that reality shall be such that personal and moral values are not accidental and without ultimate significance but rather the deepest and animating ground of all being. In brief, in the manner in which we live out such values we can exercise an existential vindication of them which is not disclosed in their conceptual representation according to which, although self-authenticating, they are constitutionally unvindicated.

This situation, according to which in the witness of life we can performatively exercise a vindication of values which seems speculatively unjustified, is exceedingly paradoxical and calls for further consideration. It suggests a train of reflection which if fully elaborated and critically justified would constitute rational grounds for an affirmation of God. Prescinding here from the difficult task of such elaboration and justification let us simply mention the bare outline of this train of thought.

We have indicated two facts which taken together may be said to constitute a paradox in that each suggests a very different appraisal of reality. On the one hand there is the fact that a reflective description of experience suggests that reality in its fundamental and ultimate characterisation is meaningless, undependable, fortuitous and brute. Although man as an intelligent free subject may be considered axio-

M

logically as an absolute value, the fact that he is at all seems ontologically quite accidental and his reality itself is undeniably precarious and contingent. Moreover, the ideal of a moral and personal order which he promotes appears to be as ontologically contingent and unvindicated as his own reality of which it is a function. On the other hand there is the fact that man can and does in the concrete exercise of his life freely commit himself to an affirmation of the ultimately personal and moral characterisation of reality. He denies the alleged ultimate absurdity of reality and enacts symbolically in a variety of social, artistic and cultural contexts the ontological primacy of meaning and value.

The clash between these opposing affirmations concerning the personal or impersonal character of the world impels one to seek a deeper understanding and more coherent appraisal of reality. In this respect a variety of possibilities suggest themselves. For example, one might argue that the world really is fundamentally impersonal and that man's attempt to deny this in action merely compounds the ultimate absurdity of being. Or one might argue that the fact of man's existential commitment to the real ultimacy of moral and personal values is somehow of itself an adequate ontological guarantee and vindication of the radically personal character of the world. Finally, one might argue that the existential claim that the world is in principle personal cannot be justified simply in terms of the intrinsic resources of the world of experience but may be justified in the light of the further affirmation of the existence of God as a personal principle transcending the finite world.

A case can certainly be made for the view that notwithstanding man's existential protest the world really is and remains fundamentally impersonal and absurd. For the freedom in virtue of which he enacts and promotes the ontological ultimacy of the personal is rooted in an encompassing context of facticity and contingency. As a contextually dependent freedom it accomplishes only a symbolic vindication of the values which it promotes, not a decisive ontological vindication of them. Hence, the ultimate absurdity and fortuitousness of all reality, including the human reality, remains an undefeated presumption.

However, this line of thought is by no means irresistible. It will scarcely convince the man who in response to the promptings of various meaningful depth-experiences commits himself existentially to the ultimately personal nature of reality and experiences such commitment as genuinely expansive of the possibilities of personal being. He will take the insistence that reality must be considered as ultimately impersonal to be an intolerable restriction and corrosion of the productive resources and exigencies of his free subjectivity. To the objection that through his existential commitment he exercises only a symbolic vindication of personal values he would reply that one must not underestimate the significance of this symbolic achievement. He would argue that it is more reasonable to interpret the symbolic vindication of the personal as a cypher of how being really is in principle than to discount entirely the significance of the symbolic achievement in a flat assertion of ultimate absurdity. As one writer observes: 'It is remarkable, for example, that men communicate with each other, form lasting and profound friendships, sometimes sacrifice themselves for one another, respect other persons quite differently from things, value creativity, build universities, and are incurably attracted by the ideal of fidelity to understanding. These facts are odd if the world of which these intelligent subjects are a part is radically absurd. . . . If man can *make* nobility and honesty relevant, the real is not quite so absurd as it seems.'[3]

Nevertheless, a genuine difficulty persists concerning the possibility of justifying the lived affirmation of the fundamentally personal and moral character of reality if in one's consideration one identifies the range of reality with the finite world of experience. For within this context the available evidence, whether of common sense, science, or philosophy, points towards the ontologically accidental, derivative, vulnerable and contingent character of the order of personal and moral values. This is the point which we have seen urged by atheistic existentialism against the various forms of optimistic humanism. It repudiates as unjustifiable any theory of history, science, or society which proclaims that the factual, raw, unstable context of man's life can be evolved through human praxis alone into an ontologically assured order of meaning and value.

A similar point is made by Wittgenstein in his early work, the *Tractatus Logico-Philosophicus*. He suggests that an affirmation of the fundamental reality of meaning and value cannot be adequately grounded within the this-worldly context of brute fact and sheer contingency. Thus he writes: 'The sense of the world must lie outside the world. In the world everything is as it is and happens as it does happen. *In* it there is no value—and if there were, it would be of no value. If there is a value which is of value, it must lie outside all happening and being-so. For all happening and being-so is accidental. What makes it non-accidental cannot lie *in* the world, for otherwise this would again be accidental. It must lie outside the world.'[4]

This suggestion that the basic principle of meaning and value must lie outside the world leads us finally to a consideration of how an affirmation of God as a personal principle transcending the finite world of human experience might advance a coherent appraisal of this world which, considered simply in itself, evokes conflicting evaluations of its meaning and value. It would appear that such an affirmation does in fact shed light upon the paradoxical activity whereby, through existential commitment, we dispute the evidence of merely speculative considerations and exercise a lived vindication of the ontological absoluteness of personal and moral values such as truth, freedom, justice and love. For it satisfies a metaphysical condition of this ontological absoluteness of these values to which we can freely witness in our activity but not really ground within ourselves or the world of our experience. This condition is the actual reality of a personal principle exercising these values in a state of ontological transcendence and independence of all situatedness, contingency and finitude. For, since these intrinsically personal values can be really operative only as originating from an intrinsically personal principle, an affirmation of their ontological absoluteness implies the ontological absoluteness of this personal principle. But if this personal principle is in fact fundamentally accidental, limited and contingent it cannot be ontologically absolute. In which case it would be inadmissible to proclaim the ontological absoluteness of the personal values themselves. For the ontologically precarious and undependable character of their personal ground would render their own ontological status fundamentally accidental, unintelligible and unvindicated. Only on the supposition that the personal principle which ultimately grounds these values is not constitutionally fortuitous and contingent can this conclusion be avoided. The reality of such a dependable principle is envisaged in the affirmation of God's transcendent personal actuality as absolute and unrestricted truth, freedom, justice and love.

Taken in this context of clarifying one's existential commitment, such an affirmation of God need not be interpreted as a source of illusion and alienation. Rather it can be seen as expressing a mystery of freedom and love, which constitutes an ontological vindication of the commitment to the ultimacy of personal and moral values exercised by man as an absolute in the order of value but constitutionally relative in the order of being. It implies that his symbolic and often costly enactment of the real primacy of the personal is meaningful and trustworthy because in harmony with the deepest ground of being.

In view of this affirmation of God as the utterly personal first principle of being, the finite world of human experience can be seen in a new light as intelligently conceived and freely intended. The phenomenon of man as finite expression and source of personal values now manifests itself as not simply a function of an encompassing pre-personal world process but also as the ephipany of a gracious divine intention. Moreover, man's various personal and moral depth-experiences can be meaningfully interpreted as not merely disclosures of human resources but also as privileged cyphers of God's infinitely personal reality. Such experiences and our inventive fidelity to their demands can be seen to have a new significance and worth as promoting the free recognition and realisation of a divinely willed personal destiny for man.

This affirmation of a divinely willed human destiny should not, as frequently occurs, be understood as compromising human freedom and creativity. For inasmuch as it is affirmed specifically as a vindication of man's free and inventive promotion of personal values it must be interpreted as preserving the seriousness and integrity of this human project. Even though it implies a reverential recognition of man's radical ontological dependence upon a more ultimate principle of meaning and value, it does not suppress his absolute value as an inherently worthwhile end in himself or his irreplaceable reality as a genuine source of original meaning and value. Man's attainment of meaning and value is not dependent upon the divine perfection in the sense that God makes naturally available to him particular items of information and moral insights which He already possesses. The divine perfection is not of the same order or realised in the same manner as human perfection. Rather it is really transcendent in relation to us.[5] Its influence in the achievement of human perfection is not discernible phenomenologically but must be understood metaphysically as enabling human subjectivity to be a self-enriching free source of a characteristically human order of meaning and value. The range and quality of this human order of meaning and value is irreplaceably a matter of the self-inventive ingenuity and moral purpose of human subjectivity. Moreover, even although through this expansion of human subjectivity one may come to acknowledge the existence of a divine perfection as one's absolute source, one is not thereby precluded or dispensed from further exercise of human creativity. For, whereas this affirmation of God may be understood to imply that reality is fundamentally such that everyone can fully and assuredly accomplish himself as a person, the actual achievement of this project of self-fulfilment is one which engages all the resources of our inventive freedom. It challenges us to freely constitute and live out an integrated ideal of personal existence involving a complex network of relationships with nature, other people, and the ultimate personal reality of God.

The brief suggestions outlined above are intended to indicate how the affirmation of God might be envisaged as both an expression of our free subjectivity and a summons to its greater self-fulfilment. The affirmation is freely, yet not irrationally, adopted as the most personalising appraisal of our freely exercised but paradoxical commitment to the ontological ultimacy and trustworthiness of personal values. Its adoption is a self-involving exercise which summons us to achieve existentially both an appropriate religious response to this divine personal ground of our subjectivity and, concomitantly, an enhanced appreciation of our secular interpersonal relationships.

It may be objected that the approach to the affirmation of God indicated here is too reliant upon the factor of man's existentially exercised options to be genuinely persuasive. God is freely affirmed as making sense of an existential option in favour of the basically personal character of reality, an option which although rationally prompted is not strictly compelled. Thus an affirmation of Him as relevant to human experience would seem to be achieved in virtue of a prior commitment to enacting experience in a manner to which such an affirmation could be relevant. A different existential response to experience, for example a response to experience which enacted experience as fundamentally absurd, fortuitous and evil, would not attain this affirmation.

The truth of this allegation might be admitted without conceding the futility of the proposed approach to God. For surely the significant consideration is not that a particular existential enactment of experience favours an affirmation of God, but the claim that this enactment of experience effects a more expansive liberation of the possibilities of personal being than does an alternative enactment of experience. The truth of this contention must ultimately be tested by each individual through reflection upon his own concretely exercised existence.

This emphasis upon the factor of existential option is a consequence of the importance attributed in modern thought to the exigencies of human freedom and autonomy. But perhaps it also highlights an important aspect of an authentic affirmation of God. For it suggests not only that God should be sought as the transcendent personal Freedom who renders finite personal freedom possible, but also that He is most authentically attained through fidelity to the exigencies of our personal freedom. In other words it suggests that God is at least as respectful of our freedom as we ourselves have become, and would have us affirm Him not lifelessly as an ineluctable necessity but only freely as the absolute personal value implicitly desired in the free commitment of our lives to the ontological primacy of the personal.

Needless to say we have left many real difficulties untouched in this outline of a possible approach to the problem of God today. It does, however, suggest a line of reflection which takes issue with the proclamation of contemporary atheism that the affirmation of God is inherently alienating and incompatible with the exigencies of human subjectivity. It suggests on the contrary that the affirmation of God can promote a more expansive liberation of the creative possibilities of human subjectivity than is available within the context of a denial of any such transcendent personal perfection. In this way it represents the affirmation of God as a hopeful project, as a goal to be joyfully anticipated and not, as the chorus of contemporary atheism proclaims, a reprehensible threat to human subjectivity.

On this note of hope we conclude this preliminary outline of a positive approach to the problem of God which has been suggested by the evolution of contemporary atheism itself. The reappearance of such hope is, as we have remarked, the necessary prolegomenon to the major philosophical enterprise of critically justifying an affirmation of God in our day.

Notes

Chapter 1

[1]J. Courtney Murray, *The Problem of God*, New Haven and London 1964. 120–21.

[2]J. Dillenberger, 'Religious Stimulants and Constraints in the Development of Science', *Continuum* (5) Spring 1967, 8.

[3]H. Butterfield, *The Origins of Modern Science 1300–1800*, London 1951, 7.

[4]A. Koyré, *From the Closed World to the Infinite Universe*, New York 1958, 276.

[5]C. Fabro, *God in Exile—Modern Atheism: A Study of the Internal Dynamic of Modern Atheism, from its Roots in the Cartesian Cogito to the Present Day*. New York 1968, 26–27.

[6]Thus, for example, Edmund Husserl the founder of phenomenology envisages his own work as following through the enterprise of Descartes and pays him the tribute that 'great weight must be given to the consideration that, in philosophy, the *Meditations* were epoch-making in a quite unique sense, and precisely because of their going back to the pure *ego cogito*. Descartes, in fact, inaugurates an entirely new kind of philosophy. Changing its total style, philosophy takes a radical turn: from naive objectivism to transcendental subjectivism—which, with its ever new but always inadequate attempts, seems to be striving towards some necessary final form, wherein its true sense and that of the radical transmutation itself might become disclosed.' E. Husserl, *Cartesian Meditations*, E. tr. D. Cairns, The Hague 1968, 4.

[7]R. Descartes, *Meditation III, The Philosophical Works of Descartes, I* (Haldane & Ross) Cambridge 1968, 165.

[8]*Ibid.*, 1966.   [9]*Ibid.*, 178.

[10]Cf. J. P. Sartre 'La liberté cartésienne', *Situations I*, Paris 1947, 314–34.

Chapter 2

[1]Cf. I. Kant, *Critique of Pure Reason*, E. tr. N. K. Smith, 2nd ed. London 1933, B 19–24.

²'Hitherto it has been assumed that all our knowledge must conform to objects. But all attempts to extend our knowledge of objects by establishing something in regard to them *a priori*, by means of concepts have, on this assumption, ended in failure. We must therefore make trial whether we may not have more success in the tasks of metaphysics, if we suppose that objects must conform to our knowledge.' *Ibid.* B XVI.

³*Ibid.*, A 125.   ⁴*Ibid.*, B 146–8.

⁵'All synthetic principles of reason allow only of an immanent employment; and in order to have knowledge of a supreme being we should have to put them to a transcendent use, for which our understanding is in no way fitted. If the empirically valid law of causality is to lead to the original being, the latter must belong to the chain of objects of experience, and in that case it would, like all appearances, be itself again conditioned.' *Ibid.* B. 664.

⁶*Ibid.*, B 672.   ⁷*Ibid.* B 730.   ⁸*Ibid.* B 628.

⁹*Ibid.* B 636. A general appraisal of Kant's critique of the proofs for God would involve an evaluation of his whole epistemological viewpoint. However, it is worth noting a specific weakness in this particular argument against the cosmological proof. Kant's objection, that to identify necessary being with *ens realissimum* is equivalently to infer necessary being from the concept of *ens realissimum* and hence relapse into the ontological argument, is not convincing. For he would not be entitled to argue as he does from 'every necessary being is an *ens realissimum*' to 'some *entia realissima* are necessary beings, if there did not exist a necessary being (as indeed the first step of the proof asserts). Hence the generalised statement 'every *ens realissimum* is a necessary being' is not really a statement of the ontological argument. Kant's reasoning shows merely that if it is correct to describe a necessary being which is known to exist as *ens realissimum* then it is correct to say that any *ens realissimum* is a necessary being. The ontological proof on the other hand is concerned with deriving *existence* from the idea of *ens realissimum*. Cf. J. Smart, 'The Existence of God', *New Essays in Philosophical Theology*, ed. Flew and MacIntyre, London 1955, 35–37.

¹⁰Kant, *op. cit.*, B 669.

¹¹This interpretation is proposed by Luijpen in the course of an interesting discussion of Kant's approach to the problem of God: cf. W. Luijpen, *Phenomenology and Atheism*, Pittsburgh 1964, 44–48.

¹²Kant, *op. cit.*, B XXX.

¹³For Kant's elaboration of this theme cf. *Critique of Pure Reason*, B 832–B 847; *Critique of Practical Reason*, E. tr. T. Abbott, 6th ed. London 1909, 202–29; *Religion within the Limits of Reason Alone*, E. tr. T. Greene and H. Hudson (Harper Torchbooks), New York 1960, *passim*.

¹⁴*Religion* . . ., 3.

¹⁵*Critique of Practical Reason*, 206.

¹⁶'We ought to endeavour to promote the *summum bonum*, which, therefore, must be possible. Accordingly, the existence of a cause of all nature, distinct from nature itself, and containing the principle of this connexion, namely, of the exact harmony of happiness with morality, is also postulated. . . . The supreme cause of nature, which must be presupposed as a condition of the

summum bonum, is a being which is the cause of nature by *intelligence* and *will,* consequently its author, that is God.' *Ibid.,* 221–2.

[17]*Ibid.,* 241.

[18]*Critique of Pure Reason,* B 857.

[19]Thus already in the *Critique of Practical Reason* he remarks that 'the Christian principle of *morality* itself is not theological (so as to be heteronomy), but is autonomy of pure practical reason, since it does not make the knowledge of God and His will the foundation of these laws, but only of the attainment of the *summum bonum,* on condition of following these laws, and it does not even place the proper *spring* of this obedience in the desired results, but solely in the conception of duty, as that of which the faithful observance alone constitutes the worthiness to obtain those happy consequences.' *Op. cit.,* 226.

[20]Cf. *Religion . . .,* 142–4.   [21]*Ibid.,* 157.   [22]*Ibid.,* 156.

[23]*Ibid.,* 158.   [24]Cf. *Ibid.,* 145–51.   [25]Cf. *ibid.,* 179–90.

[26]*Ibid.,* 159.

[27]A. Kenny, *The Five Ways: St Thomas Aquinas' Proofs of God's Existence,* London 1969, 3.

[28]It is perhaps interesting to note that the work in which Francis Jeanson elaborates his rejection of religious belief is entitled *La foi d'un incroyant,* Paris 1963.

Chapter 3

[1]The first two parts of *The Positivity of the Christian Religion* were written in 1795–96. The third part, a greatly revised version of some of the earlier text, was written in 1800. *The Spirit of Christianity and its Fate* was written in 1798–99. These, together with other early writings unpublished by Hegel, have been translated from Hegel's *Theologische Jugendschriften,* ed. H. Nohl, Tübingen 1907, by T. Knox and R. Kroner in *On Christianity: Early Theological Writings by Friedrich Hegel* (Harper Torchbooks), New York 1961.

[2]*On Christianity . . . ,* 69–71   [3]*Ibid.,* 173.   [4]*Ibid.,* 175.

[5]*Ibid.,* 176.   [6]*Ibid.,* 68.   [7]*Ibid.,* 211.

[8]*Ibid.,* 212.   [9]*Ibid.,* 247.   [10]*Ibid.,* 313.

[11]Cf. the section on Romanticism in R. Kroner's valuable Introduction to *On Christianity,* 14–28.

[12]The chief source of the following account of Hegel's philosophical discussion of God and religion is his *Lectures on Philosophy of Religion.* They comprise courses given between 1821 and 1831 and compiled posthumously from his own notes and copies of the lectures made by some of his pupils. Quotations are from the English version *Lectures on the Philosophy of Religion (Together with a Work on the Proofs of the Existence of God),* E. tr. E. B. Spiers and J. B. Sanderson (3 vols.), London, 1895 (reprinted 1968). Cf. *Samanthlicke Werke,* ed. H. Glockner, Stuttgart 1927–39, vols. XV & XVI.

[13]A critical evaluation of Hegel's procedure could indicate a circular relationship between his philosophy of spirit and this master principle which determines his fundamental requirement of an authentic philosophical system.

If the logical categories of human enquiry are identical with the laws of being (more traditionally, if there is ultimately an absolute correspondence between the *quoad nos* and the *quoad se*) then the ideal, envisaged in his philosophy, of total reflection yielding an adequate exposition of the creative thought of an all-embracing absolute spirit might, in principle, be achieved. But it could be argued that the alleged equivalence between the real and human rationality can be sustained only if the doctrine of absolute spirit is in fact presupposed and man can indeed know the unfolding of events from a divine point of view. While Hegel might rejoice in this circularity as quite consistent with 'the resolve that wills pure thought' there remains the possible objection that the transcendent perfection of the real order and the limitations which affect man's cognitional access to it require a radically different metaphysics and a more modest conception of philosophical system. Cf. J. Collins, *God in Modern Philosophy*, Chicago 1959, 210–11.

[14]*Philosophy of Religion*, I, 174.

[15]*Ibid.*, III, 164.

[16]J. Collins, *The Emergence of Philosophy of Religion*, New Haven 1967, 298.

[17]*Philosophy of Religion*, I. 200.

[18]*Ibid.*, I, 198.

[19]*Ibid.*, I, 199–200.

[20]*The Logic of Hegel—Translated from the Encyclopaedia of the Philosophical Sciences*, E. tr. W. Wallace, 2nd ed. Oxford 1892 (reprinted 1968), par. 163.

[21]*Philosophy of Religion*, I, 198.

[22]For a classical exposition of this viewpoint cf. St Thomas Aquinas, *Summa Theologiae*, I, q. 19, a. 3, and I, q. 44, a. 4.

[23]Cf. *ibid.*, I, q. 3, *passim*.

[24]'The human, the finite, frailty, weakness, the negative, is itself a divine moment, is in God Himself; otherness or Other-Being, the finite, the negative, is not outside of God, and in its character as otherness it does not hinder unity with God; otherness, the negation, is consciously known to be a moment of the Divine nature. The highest knowledge of the nature of the Idea of Spirit is contained in this thought.' *Philosophy of Religion*, III, 98.

[25]Cf. St Thomas Aquinas, *op. cit.*, I, q. 10, *passim*.

[26]*Philosophy of Religion*, III, 1.

[27]*Ibid.*, III, 37.   [28]*Ibid.*, III, 10.   [29]*Ibid.*, III, 42.

[30]For a penetrating version of such an interpretation cf. G. Van Riet, 'Le problème de Dieu chez Hegel. Athéisme ou christianisme?' *Revue Philosophique de Louvain*, tome 63, 1965, 353–418. Cf. also E. Fackenheim's masterly study, *The Religious Dimension in Hegel's Thought*, Bloomington and London 1967, chs. 5–7.

[31]'The possibility of reconciliation rests only on the conscious recognition of the implicit unity of divine and human nature; this is the necessary basis. Thus Man can know that he has been received into union with God in so far as God is not for him something foreign to his nature, in so far as he does not stand related to God as an external accident, but when he has been taken up into God in his essential character in a way which is in accordance with his freedom

and subjectivity; this, however, is possible only in so far as this subjectivity which belongs to human nature exists in God Himself.' *Philosophy of Religion*, III, 71.

[32]J. Collins. *The Emergence of Philosophy of Religion*, 279.

[33]'The rise of thought beyond the world of sense, its passage from the finite to the infinite, the leap into the super-sensible which it takes when it snaps asunder the chain of sense, all this transition is thought and nothing but thought. . . . Animals make no such transition. They never get further than sensation and the perception of the senses, and in consequence they have no religion.' *Logic of Hegel*, par. 50; cf. also *Philosophy of Religion*, I, 160–172.

[34]*Philosophy of Religion*, I, 206.

[35]For a discussion of this complex term *Vorstellung* cf. *ibid.*, I, 142–5.

[36]Cf. G. Hegel, *The Phenomenology of Mind*, E. tr. J. B. Baillie, London 1931, 229–67.

[37]*Philosophy of Religion*, II, 340.

[38]Cf. *ibid.*, II, 209–219.   [39]*Ibid.*, II, 211.

[40]'The conscious perception of the unity of the soul with the Absolute, or of the reception of the soul into the bosom of the Absolute, has not yet arisen. Man has as yet no inner space, no inner extension, no soul of such an extent as to lead it to wish for satisfaction within itself, but rather it is the temporal which gives it fullness and reality.' *Ibid.*, II, 213.

[41]*Ibid.*, III, 76–77.   [42]*Ibid.*, III, 86–100.

[43]'This death is love itself, expressed as a moment of God, and it is this death which brings about reconciliation. In it we have a picture of absolute love. It is the identity of the Divine and the human, it implies that in the finite God is at home with Himself, and this finite as seen in death is itself a determination belonging to God. God has through death reconciled the world, and reconciled it eternally with Himself. This coming back from the state of estrangement is His return to Himself, and it is because of it that He is Spirit.' *Ibid.*, III, 96.

[44]*Ibid.*, III, 138.   [45]*Ibid.*, I, 257.

[46]Cf. *ibid.*, III, 105.   [47]*Ibid.*, I, 247.

[48]'In faith the true content is certainly already found, but there is still wanting to it the form of thought. All forms such as we have already dealt with, feeling, popular ideas, and such like, may certainly have the form of truth, but they themselves are not the true form which makes the true content necessary. Thought is the absolute judge before which the content must verify and attest its claims.' *Ibid.*, III, 148.

[49]*Ibid.*, III, 121–122.

[50]Cf. R. Vancourt, *La pensée religieuse de Hegel*, Paris 1965, 104–6.

Chapter 4

[1]L. Feuerbach, *The Essence of Christianity*, E. tr. George Eliot (Marian Evans), Introd. K. Barth, Foreword H. R. Niebuhr (Harper Torchbook), New York 1957, xii.

[2]*Ibid.*, 131–14.   [3]*Ibid.*, 3.   [4]*Ibid.*, 5.
[5]*Ibid.*, 5.   [6]*Ibid.*, 33.   [7]*Ibid.*, 230.
[8]*Ibid.*, 5.   [9]*Ibid.*, 15.   [10]Cf. *ibid.*, 17–19.
[11]*Ibid.*, 19.

[12]'The essence of religion is the immediate, involuntary, unconscious contemplation of the human nature as another, a distinct nature. But when this projected image of human nature is made an object of reflection, of theology, it becomes an inexhaustible mine of falsehoods, illusions, contradictions, and sophisms.' *Ibid.*, 213–14.

[13]*Ibid.*, 45.

[14]*Ibid.*, 53.   [15]*Ibid.*, 67.   [16]*Ibid.*, 79.
[17]*Ibid.*, 83.   [18]*Ibid.*, 184.   [19]*Ibid.*, 152.

[20]Cf. *ibid.*, 150–59. Needless to say this doctrine of man as a species being has been one of the most influential features of Feuerbach's thought. In particular it has exercised a profound influence on the development of Marx's conception of man as a social being.

[21]Cf. *ibid.*, 156.   [22]*Ibid.*, 158.   [23]*Ibid.*, 159.
[24]Cf. *Ibid.*, 277.

[25]This point is well developed by C. Fabro—cf. *God in Exile*, 650–71.

[26]E. Kamenka, *The Philosophy of Ludwig Feuerbach*, London 1970, 109.

[27]'The mystery of the inexhaustible fullness of the divine predicates is therefore nothing else than the mystery of human nature considered as an infinitely varied, infinitely modifiable, but, consequently, phenomenal being.' *The Essence of Christianity*, 23.

Chapter 5.

[1]'Philosophy makes no secret of it. Prometheus's admission "I hate all gods" is its own admission, its own motto against all gods, heavenly and earthly, who do not acknowledge the consciousness of man as the supreme divinity.' From the Foreword to Marx's thesis: *The Difference between the Natural Philosophy of Democritus and the Natural Philosophy of Epicurus*, translated in K. Marx and F. Engels, *On Religion*, Moscow 1955, 15.

[2]K. Marx, *Economic and Philosophical Manuscripts* (referred to henceforth as *EPM*), translated by T. B. Bottomore in *Karl Marx—Early Writings*. London 1963, 166.

[3]K. Marx, *Contribution to the Critique of Hegel's Philosophy of Right*, Introd. *Early Writings*, 43.

[4]*Ibid.*, 44.   [5]*Ibid.*, 43.   [6]*Ibid.*, 43.

[7]Cf. K. Marx, *The Communism of the Paper Rheinischer Beobachter, On Religion*, 83–84.

[8]*EPM* III, *Early Writings*, 165.

[9]*Contribution to the Critique of Hegel's Philosophy of Right, Early Writings*, 44.

[10]*Ibid.*, 59.

[11]K. Marx and F. Engels, *German Ideology*, ch. I, *On Religion*, 70.

[12]*EPM* I, *Early Writings*, 130.

[13]*EPM* III, *Early Writings*, 156.

[14]*Contribution to the Critique of Hegel's Philosophy of Right*, *Early Writings*, 58.

[15]Cf. *German Ideology*, ch. I, *On Religion*, 73–81.

[16]*Contribution to the Critique of Hegel's Philosophy of Right*, *Early Writings*, 44.

[17]*EPM* III, *Early Writings*, 166.

[18]*German Ideology*, ch. I, *On Religion*, 74–5.

[19]Cf. *EPM* I, *Early Writings*, 120–34.

[20]*EPM* III, *Early Writings*, 164–5.

[21]*Ibid.*, 160.   [22]Cf. *ibid.*, 158–9.   [23]*Ibid.*, 157.

[24]*Ibid.*, 158.   [25]*Ibid.*, 155.   [26]*Ibid.*, 166–7.

[27]*Ibid.*, 176.

[28]Cf. J. Ladrière, *Anthropologie du Marxisme et le Marxisme Sovietique*, Brussels 1962, 58–9.

[29]Cf. D. Turner, *On the Philosophy of Karl Marx*, Dublin 1968, 62–8.

[30]'It is above all necessary to avoid postulating "society" once again as an abstraction confronting the individual. The individual *is* the *social being.*' *EPM* III, *Early Writings*, 158.

[31]*Ibid.*, 158.

[32]Cf. J. Ladrière, 'History and Destiny', *Philosophy Today*, V (1965), 22–4.

Chapter 6

[1]D. Hume, *Enquiries Concerning the Human Understanding and Concerning the Principles of Morals*, ed. Selby-Bigge, 2nd ed. Oxford 1962, 2, 17.

[2]For an interesting discussion of eighteenth-century French atheistic materialism, cf. C. Fabro, *God in Exile*, 361–487.

[3]F. Copleston, *A History of Philosophy*, VI, London 1960, 4.

[4]*The Positive Philosophy of Auguste Comte*, translated and condensed by H. Martineau, 2 vols, London 1853, vol. I, 2.

[5]'The consideration of all phenomena as referable to a single origin is by no means necessary to the systematic formation of science, any more than to the realisation of the great and happy consequences that we anticipate from the positive philosophy. The only necessary unity is that of Method, which is already in great part achieved.' *Ibid.*, 17.

[6]*Ibid.*, 8.

[7]For an account of the new religion of Humanity, cf. A. Comte, *A General View of Positivism*, E. tr. J. H. Bridges, London 1865, 340–426.

[8]Cf. H. de Lubac, *The Drama of Atheist Humanism*, E. tr. E. Riley, Cleveland and New York 1963, 150–59.

[9]*Ibid.*, 82.

[10]Cf. J. Dewey, *A Common Faith*, New Haven 1934.

[11]Cf. C. Lévi-Strauss, *The Scope of Anthropology*, E. tr. O. and F. Paul, London, 1967.

[12]The following discussion of contemporary linguistic philosophy in its bearing upon the problem of God is indebted to the admirable study by F. Ferré, *Language Logic and God*, London 1962.

[13]Cf. A. J. Ayer, *Language Truth and Logic*, 2nd ed., London 1946, ch. 1.

[14]*Ibid.*, 115.

[15]In this context it may be worth observing that Freud too can be considered as belonging to the tradition of positivistic naturalism inasmuch as he correlates religious belief with illusion, childishness and alienation, and suggests that this infantile state of humanity can be transcended chiefly through the progress of science. Cf. S. Freud, *The Future of an Illusion*, E. tr. W. D. Robson-Scott, London 1949.

[16]Cf. F. Ferré, *Language Logic and God*, 42–57.

[17]Cf. L. Wittgenstein, *Philosophical Investigations*, E. tr. E. Anscombe, 2nd ed. Oxford 1958, 11e-12e.

[18]Together with F. Ferré's *Language Logic and God*, one might mention as examples of such work D. Evans, *The Logic of Self-Involvement*, London 1963 and New York 1969; and P. Geach, *God and the Soul*, London 1969.

[19]D. Evans, *The Logic of Self-Involvement*, 24.

[20]A. N. Prior, 'Can Religion be Discussed?' *New Essays in Philosophical Theology*, ed. A. Flew and A. MacIntyre, London 1955, 5–6.

[21]I. M. Crombie, 'Theology and Falsification', *ibid.*, 113–14.

[22]Cf. the discussion of A. Flew, R. M. Hare, B. Mitchell and I. M. Crombie on this topic in 'Theology and Falsification', *ibid.*, 96–130.

[23]Thus Aquinas observes: 'Since we come to know God from creatures and since this is how we come to refer to him, the expressions we use to name him signify in a way appropriate to the material creatures we ordinarily know. Amongst such creatures the complete subsistent thing is always a concrete union of form and matter; for the form itself is not a subsistent thing, but that by which something subsists. Because of this the words we use to signify complete subsistent things are concrete nouns which are appropriate to composite subjects. When, on the other hand, we want to speak of the form itself we use abstract nouns which do not signify something as subsistent, but as that by which something is: 'whiteness', for example, signifies the form as that by which something is white.

'Now God is both simple, like the form, and subsistent, like the concrete thing, and so we sometimes refer to him by abstract nouns to indicate his simplicity and sometimes by concrete nouns to indicate his subsistence and completeness; though neither way of speaking measures up to his way of being, for in this life we do not know him as he is in himself.' *Summa Theologiae*, I, q. 13, a. 1, ad 2; E. tr. vol. 3, London 1964, 49–51.

[24]Cf. *ibid.*, I, q. 3, a. 3, ad 1; and I, q. 13, a. 3.

[25]Cf. A. Rainier, 'Can God's Existence be Disproved?' *New Essays in Philosophical Theology*, 67–8; and W. Norris Clarke, 'Linguistic Analysis and Natural Theology' *Proceedings of the American Philosophical Association*, XXXIV (1960), 115–20.

N

[26]G. Anscombe and P. Geach, *Three Philosophers*, Oxford 1961, 114.

[27]'Does anything count against the assertion that God is merciful? . . . Yes, suffering which was utterly, eternally and irredeemably pointless. Can we then design a crucial experiment? No, because we can never see all of the picture. Two things at least are hidden from us; what goes on in the recesses of the personality of the sufferer, and what shall happen hereafter.' I. Crombie, 'Theology and Falsification', *New Essays in Philosophical Theology*, 124–5; cf. also J. Hick, *Faith and Knowledge*, New York 1957, 155–61; and F. Copleston, *Contemporary Philosophy*, London 1956, 100–101.

[28]W. Norris Clarke, 'Analytic Philosophy and Language about God', *Christian Philosophy and Religious Renewal*, ed. G. McLean, Washington 1966, 59.

[29]A. Flew, *God and Philosophy*, London 1966, 3.20.

[30]Cf. *ibid.*, 3.20–3.30.

[31]'All our knowledge of things, of their natures and tendencies, has to be founded upon and checked against the ways those things in fact behave, under whatever conditions they can be available for our study. Yet, if this is so, is it not topsy-turvy to insist that those things cannot naturally do what is, in our experience, precisely what they do do?' *Ibid.*, 3.25.

[32]Cf. *ibid.*, 4.34.   [33]Cf. *ibid.*, 4.18.   [34]Cf. *ibid.*, 4.37–4.39.
[35]*Ibid.*, 9.29.

[36]Cf. P. J. McGrath, 'Professor Flew and the Stratonician Presumption', *Philosophical Studies*, XVIII (1969), 151.

[37]P. J. McGrath's article provides an interesting expansion of the points which we have mentioned. Cf. *ibid.*, 150–59.

[38]A. Flew, *God and Philosophy*, 9.27.

[39]Cf. J. Ladrière, 'Crisis of Civilization—Crisis of Institution', *Convergence*, P.R.J., I (1970), 3–8.

Chapter 7

[1]M. Merleau-Ponty, *Phenomenology of Perception*, E. tr. C. Smith, London 1962, ix.

[2]For an illuminating exposition and critical analysis of the main features of Jaspers' philosophy cf. S. Samay, *Reason Revisited: The Philosophy of Karl Jaspers*, Dublin 1971.

[3]A valuable selection of Nietzsche's writings is conveniently available in *The Portable Nietzsche*, translated, edited and with a critical introduction by W. Kaufmann, New York 1968.

[4]For a lucid résumé of his basic philosophical position cf. J.P. Sartre, *Existentialism and Humanism*, E. tr. and Introduction by P. Mairet, London 1948.

[5]Cf. *ibid.*, 51–5.

[6]Thus in one of Sartre's plays Orestes proclaims to Jupiter: 'What have I to do with you or you with me? We shall glide past each other, like ships in a river, without touching. You are God and I am free; each of us is alone, and our anguish is akin.' J.P. Sartre, *The Flies*, New York 1947, 159.

[7]Cf. J.P. Sartre, *Existentialism and Humanism*, 26-7.

[8]*Ibid.*, 33-4.

[9]Cf. J.P. Sartre, *Being and Nothingness: An Essay on Phenomenological Ontology*, E. tr. and Introduction by H. E. Barnes, Washington Square Press edition, New York 1966, 724-5.

[10]For a brief but incisive elaboration of these considerations cf. the chapter entitled 'Sartre's Postulatory Atheism' in J. Collins, *The Existentialists: A Critical Study*, Chicago 1952.

[11]'Everything happens therefore as if the in-itself and the for-itself were presented in a state of disintegration in relation to an ideal synthesis. Not tha the integration has ever *taken place* but on the contrary because it is alway indicated and always impossible.' J.P. Sartre, *Being and Nothingness*, 792. The radical opposition which Sartre proclaims between the in-itself and the for-itself is at the root of various other objections, not entered into here, which he raises in this study against the coherence of any affirmation of God.

[12]*Ibid.*, 784.

[13]'We are involved in the world and with others in an inextricable tangle. The idea of situation rules out absolute freedom at the source of our commitments, and equally indeed at their terminus.' M. Merleau-Ponty, *Phenomenology of Perception*, 454.

[14]'As long as we place in opposition, with no mediator, the For-Itself and the In-Itself and fail to perceive, between ourselves and the world, this natural foreshadowing of a subjectivity, . . . everything becomes equally a matter of choice, the respiratory reflex no less than the moral decision, conservation no less than creation.' *Ibid.*, 453.

[15]Cf. M. Merleau-Ponty, *Éloge de la Philosophie*, 14e édition, Paris 1953, 58-63.

[16]This problem of articulating comprehensible 'God-talk' is one which affects not only dialogue between believers and unbelievers but also, as the literature of 'death-of-God theology' and 'secular-Christianity' illustrates, the attempts of believers to give an account even to themselves of their own belief. Cf. J. Robinson, *Honest to God*, London 1963, T. Altizer and W. Hamilton, *Radical Theology and the Death of God*, London 1961; L. Dewart, *The Future of Belief*, New York 1966.

[17]Cf. the chapter entitled 'The Atheism of Merleau-Ponty' in the excellent study of Merleau-Ponty's philosophy by R. Kwant, *The Phenomenological Philosophy of Merleau-Ponty*, Pittsburgh 1963, 128-49.

[18]Cf. M. Merleau-Ponty, *Éloge de la Philosophie*, 61.

[19]Cf. *ibid.*, 61-2.

[20]Cf. R. Kwant, *The Phenomenological Philosophy of Merleau-Ponty*, 299-301.

[21]'But since, on the contrary, we are in the world, since indeed our reflections are carried out in the temporal flux on to which we are trying to seize (since they *sich einstromen*, as Husserl says), there is no thought which embraces all thought.' *Phenomenology of Perception*, xiv.

[22]*Ibid.*, 170-71.

[23]Cf. *ibid.*, 365.

[24]Cf. R. Kwant, *The Phenomenological Philosophy of Merleau-Ponty*, 96–127.

[25]'This certainty which we enjoy of reaching, beyond expression, a truth separable from it and of which expression is merely the garment and contingent manifestation, has been implanted in us precisely by language.' *Phenomenology of Perception*, 401.

[26]'Ontological contingency, the contingency of the world itself, being radical, is what forms the basis once and for all of our ideas of truth.' *Ibid.*, 398.

[27]Thus Merleau-Ponty observes that the contingency of everything that exists and of everything of value is not an insignificant truth to be somehow accommodated within a system but rather the fundamental condition of any genuinely metaphysical view of the world. Cf. 'Le metaphysique dans l'homme', *Sens et non-sens*, 3e édition, Paris 1961, 168.

[28]Cf. 'Foi et bonne foi', *Sens et non-sens*, 305–321. In this essay Merleau-Ponty seeks to explain the mercurial impression which, he alleges, Catholics present to the world. He argues that it results from their dilemma of trying to operate an incoherent concept of God involving both the Father beyond the world and the Son incarnate in the world. Because of this their attitude to the world is ambivalent, an unproductive dialectic of indifference and commitment. They are a living ambiguity—in the world but not of it. They have no sense of the opportune moment or feeling for the world's future. They are both bad conservatives and bad revolutionaries and hence are not to be relied upon.

[29]Cf. M. Merleau-Ponty, 'Le metaphysique dans l'homme', *Sens et non-sens*, 166–7.

[30]Cf. *ibid.*, 167.

[31]'Thus we understand that rebellion cannot exist without a strange form of love. Those who find no rest in God or in history are condemned to live for those who, like themselves, cannot live: in fact, for the humiliated.' A. Camus, *The Rebel*, E. tr. A. Bower, (Peregrine Books,) London 1962, 268.

[32]A. Camus, *The Plague*, E. tr. S. Gilbert, 'The Collected Fiction of Albert Camus', London 1960, 144.

[33]*Ibid.*, 144.

[34]Cf. F. Jeanson, *La foi d'un incroyant*, Paris 1963.

[35]'Je crois qu'il ne faut croire qu'à ce qu'on parie de réaliser.' *ibid.*, 183.

[36]J.P. Sartre, *Being and Nothingness*, 24.

[37]'I am the absolute source, my existence does not stem from my antecedents, from my physical and social environment; instead it moves out towards them and sustains them, for I alone bring into being for myself (and therefore into being in the only sense that the word can have for me) the tradition which I elect to carry on.' M. Merleau-Ponty, *Phenomenology of Perception*, ix.

[38]Thus Merleau-Ponty remarks that one is entitled to consider as ultimate and true the contradictions of one's life as a thinking subject yet incarnate, as finite yet capable of truth, because these are features of our experience and they combine together harmoniously in our perception of things and in our experience of truths. Cf. 'Le metaphysique dans l'homme', *Sens et non-sens*, 169.

[39]For a development of this theme cf. A. Dondeyne, *Contemporary European Thought and Christian Faith*, E. tr. E. McMullin and J. Burnheim, Pittsburgh 1962, 108–25.

[40]J.P. Sartre, *Existentialism and Humanism*, 33–4.

[41]A. Camus, *The Rebel*, 226–9.

Chapter 8

[1]Cf. J. Girardi, 'Athéisme et théisme face au problème de la valeur absolue de l'homme', *Revue Philosophique de Louvain*, tome 65 (1967), 207–25.

[2]For a valuable discussion of such depth-experiences cf. D. Evans, 'Differences between Scientific and Religious Assertions', *Science and Religion*, ed. I. Barbour, London 1968, 101–33.

[3]M. Novak, *Belief and Unbelief*, London 1966, 145.

[4]L. Wittgenstein, *Tractatus Logico-Philosophicus*, London 1922, 6.41.

[5]Cf. G. Verbeke, 'Christian Faith and Philosophical Research', *Studies*, LV (1966), 120–30.

Index

187